Remembering
Who You Truly Are

Remembering Who You Truly Are

A Spirit-Lifting Daily Guide

G. Richard Rieger

SpiritLifting Publications

Illustrations by Deborah Waddington Smith

Cover photo copyright David Muench

ISBN: 0-9760740-0-1

Library of Congress Control Number: 2004097349

Online

These Day Book Messages can be found at:

www.spiritlifting.com

This site also offers other inspirational materials, CDs, books, and videos.

Online spiritual counseling and career/life coaching can also be arranged with the author through the website.

Spirit-Lifting Publications

18 Schrier Avenue

Salem, NJ 08079

856.935.6781

Dedication

I dedicate this book to Marilyn, my beloved wife,
best friend, and co-worker, who led me into my life's work
and continues to believe in me.
Although she has passed from this Earth,
she continues to inspire me from the spiritual side of life.
Many of her inspirational radio scripts and website messages
are included in this book.

Acknowledgments

My thanks to:

—my dear friends, Mary-Alice and Richard Jafolla, successful published authors in their own right, who did the initial proofreading and brainstormed with me on many aspects of the book, including title and publishing.

—my editors and book packagers, Linda and Jim Salisbury for their fine professional efforts, and friendly counseling on the publishing of the book.

—Deborah Waddington Smith, professional sculptor and artist, whose original artwork illustrates the daily messages so beautifully.

—the encouragement of my many friends, especially Joyce Browne, Mary Waddington, and Linda and Bruce Koe.

—the review and suggestions of my friends in the Pendle Hill Creative Writing Workshop, and the professional advice of Tom Mullen, Leader of the Pendle Hill Workshop.

—to my angels and loved ones on the invisible side of life for their inspiration.

How To Use *GOD'S DAY BOOK*

The purpose of this Daybook is to—
(1) help you awaken to the Presence of God within you.
(2) help you remember who you really are—a spiritual being,
a beloved expression of God, one with all life.

On every page you will find answers for the problems
you face in your daily life. A subject index lists spiritual topics
for ready reference: healing, prosperity, relationships, career, etc.

Since every day is God's Day you can begin God's Daybook at anytime of the year, or just slip your finger into the book
at random for inspiration.

To help you remember the truth about yourself each page
begins with:

Remember,_____,
          (speak your name aloud)

Speak your own name aloud in the blank space, and read
the message as if you were speaking the spiritual truths to
yourself. Your own name carries its own powerful vibrations, as
do the prayers you speak aloud each day.

At the bottom of every page is an opportunity to be grateful
in some way:

TODAY, I AM GRATEFUL FOR: _____

_____

Developing a habit of moment-by-moment gratitude is one
of the master keys to happiness.

Remember, every day is GOD'S DAY,
rejoice and be glad in it!

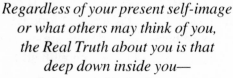

THE TRUTH ABOUT YOURSELF

Regardless of your present self-image
or what others may think of you,
the Real Truth about you is that
deep down inside you—
—beneath the outer shell of your personality,
—beyond any childhood scars and traumas,
—beyond any lack of education, or past failures,
or the limitations of your present circumstances—

Beyond all of that outer, is your Real Self,
the unique being that your Creator created you to be—
strong, capable, wise and worth loving.
You are a unique and valuable individual.

You are an eternal being,
now in the process of awakening to your True Potential.

The process may at times, seem tedious, or even hopeless.
It may seem too much to bear, too discouraging.
But know this much truly that while you may fail
if you try to "go it alone," the Power and Intelligence of your
Creator's Presence in the heart of you cannot fail.

You will succeed, as you rely on your
Higher Power moment-by-moment one day at a time.
It is never too late to begin again, because it is never too late
to forgive yourself and others and release the past.

The Mark of Success is upon you!
Hold firm to this idea,
and rededicate and reconsecrate yourself
to letting that True Self express and work through you.

Your new Good is now being prepared for you.
Give life the Light touch!
Go with the flow of Spirit, and be grateful!

GOD'S DAY 1 — *Barnacles of the Soul*

Remember, _____,
(speak your name aloud)

*—as you sail through life you
accumulate barnacles on your soul
that, like those on the hull of a ship,
weigh you down and slow your
progress.*

Your barnacles are the old
unhappy memories, guilts, resentments, and self-defeating
attitudes that have accumulated over the years.

Start the new year by going into "dry-dock" to have the
barnacles scraped off the hull of your soul.

Take time to go into prayer and meditation now and ask
God to help you clear your soul of these past accumulations, and
help you to forgive and be freed of them.

In prayer scan your memory to find these old barnacles.
Look back over your life, your relationships, and childhood.
Find the hard scars and attitudes that cling to your soul and
weigh heavy on your heart.

Let your prayer be:

*Loving Lord, I am ready to forgive and be forgiven.
Help me now to clear my soul
of these old hurts, fears, and resentments.
With your love, heal my heart of these old scars.
Restore my soul. Thy loving will be done.*

*TODAY, I AM GRATEFUL FOR:*_____

_____

GOD'S DAY 2 — New Beginnings

Remember,_____,
                   (speak your name aloud)

—a new year is like a brand new car—all shiny, loaded with
power and new gadgets and just waiting to be driven!
Get in and turn the key!

Where do you want to go?

What new roads do you want to explore?

What would you really love to do and be?

What would you really love to achieve?

In your quiet time now, write out your soul's sincerest desires for this new year shining before you.

Let the answers come from deep within you. Know they are part of that which you came into this world to accomplish. They are Spirit-directed and true.

In prayer now, ask God to be your Inner Partner in achieving these desires.

Invite God to be your Navigator for your journey.

Take a notepad and write the following questions:

Where do I want to go?

What new roads do I want to explore?

What would I really love to do and be?

What would I really love to achieve?

Sit quietly and let the answers flow into your mind.

TODAY, I AM GRATEFUL FOR: _____

_____

GOD'S DAY 3 — *Guidance*

Remember,_____,
> (speak your name aloud)

—to listen for guidance from your Navigator today.

That Voice of Wisdom is saying to you now:

> *I Am the Power within you that can break old habits.*
> *I Am the Power within you that can attain*
> *your highest aspirations.*

Continue describing and defining your soul's highest
aspirations. Test them to see if they are sincere, pure, and honest.
If so, they are Spirit-directed. You came into this world already
programmed to achieve them. They are part of your spiritual
DNA.

> *Let these words of E.C. Hopkins encourage you:*
> *"Your highest aspiration is that which you are intended to fulfill,*
> *and if you have heretofore let any environments or*
> *circumstances*
> *sap your confidence in your aspirations,*
> *it is time you pruned your ideas...*
> *" 'I am the True Vine. The way I begin to reign in you is when*
> *you trust your highest aspirations, your only hope,*
> *and prune boldly the tremblings of apprehension,*
> *of short-sightedness, of prophecies of evil.*
> *'Nothing shall prevail against me,' says Jesus Christ,*
> *in man the hope of glory.*
> *"Trust your hope. Never mind who tells you the particulars*
> *of downfall or disaster—trust your hope.*
> *It is a branch from the deathless soul*
> *that dwells in you as the true vine or true creation of God . . ."*[1]

*TODAY, I AM GRATEFUL FOR:*_____

_____

GOD'S DAY 4 — *Harmony*

Remember,_____,
          (speak your name aloud)

          —to get in tune with the Infinite today.

Think of a great symphony orchestra. Before the conductor comes out, each musician is tuning up— plucking, drumming, and tooting. The resultant sound is a jumbled mass of noise!

Then, seemingly from out of nowhere, an "A" note is sounded, and every instrument tunes to it. The conductor appears and gives the signal to begin. Beautiful, harmonious music comes forth, easily and without strain.

Today, take time to get *in tune* with the Spirit of Life within you. In the midst of outer turmoil and stress, know there is a note of perfect harmony with the Infinite sounding within you.

From this center of harmony speak these words to yourself:

          I walk without hurry,
          I work without strain.
          I live without aging,
          For I am in tune with the Infinite!

TODAY, I AM GRATEFUL FOR: _____

_____

GOD'S DAY 5 — *True Identity*

Remember,_____,
        (speak your name aloud)

*   —there is a greater Identity beyond this one*
that you think you are.

There is another greater Life beyond this one you think you are living.

There is another more beautiful Love beyond this one you feel in your heart now.

There is another Reality beyond this reality that you are aware of.

Be willing to let go of the lesser to move into the Greater.

In your quiet time now, meditate on this prayer:

Beloved Lord, show me the Greater today.
I surrender the lesser that I may experience the Greater,
the Infinite, the All-Loving.
Let there be no more me,
and only You living, loving, shining!

*TODAY, I AM GRATEFUL FOR:*_____

_____

GOD'S DAY 6 — God Can Handle It

Remember,_____,
    (speak your name aloud)

—there is nothing you will face today
that God cannot handle.

There is no burden too heavy that God's strength in you cannot bear.

There is no problem that the wisdom of God in you cannot solve.

There is no break-up, no falling-out, that God's Love cannot reconcile.

There is no disease that God's Love cannot heal.

No matter how hopeless the situation, the Power of God can handle it.

In your meditation now, call to mind the difficulty that is disturbing you, and give it to God to handle.

Let your prayer be:

Loving Lord, Here is this burden.
I give this entire situation into your loving care.
Thank You.

TODAY, I AM GRATEFUL FOR: _____

_____

GOD'S DAY 7 — *Deeper Meaning*

Remember, _____,
(speak your name aloud)

*—to look for the deeper meanings
in the things you do today.*

When you straighten out your bed in the morning, think of straightening out your mind—getting it in order, ready for the new day.

When you take your morning shower think of washing away the old thoughts and regrets of yesterday so that you are ready for the new day.

Myrtle Fillmore, co-founder of the Unity prayer movement, liked to look beyond the outer to find deeper meaning in every day experiences. In her day women did a lot of ironing. She suggested they regard that activity as ironing out the inharmonies in their family and personal relationships, making them smooth and harmonious.

So, remember, as you move through this day see the deeper purpose and meaning behind the routine activities you engage in. It will make your life more meaningful and more joyous!

In your meditation now, visualize the routine daily activities ahead of you. Find the hidden metaphors in them, and bless them.

TODAY, I AM GRATEFUL FOR: _____

GOD'S DAY 8 — Gratitude

Remember,_____,
         (speak your name aloud)

  *—you are standing on the shoulders of all those
  who have helped you up the mountain path of life.*

Be grateful.

Today, in your quiet time, look back down the path all the way to the bottom of the mountain—to childhood.

Thank those who gave you birth, and those who supported you, and encouraged you in your youth.

Thank also those who made life difficult for you—for they helped you to learn hard lessons you needed to learn.

Thank those further up the path of life who taught you and befriended you, and those that loved you.

You are where you are today because of all of these.

Be grateful today, and help someone else up the mountain path of their life.

TODAY, I AM GRATEFUL FOR: _____

_____

GOD'S DAY 9 — *God in Charge*

Remember, _____,

(speak your name aloud)

—first things first!

Begin today by turning to God and inviting that One Presence and Power to take charge of your day.

As you set out in your car, send the Spirit of God ahead to make safe and easy your way.

Before beginning a work project, ask for God's guidance and blessing upon your work.

As you fall off to sleep at night, ask God to renew and restore your body temple while you rest.

In your quiet time now, make that connection.

Ask God to direct your activities today and arrange them in divine order and sequence. Visualize your Inner Partner working with you in all that you do.

Let your prayer be:

Loving Spirit, this is Your day.
Guide and direct me as I walk through it.

*TODAY, I AM GRATEFUL FOR:*_____

_____

GOD'S DAY 10 — *Light-Bearer*

Remember, _____,
(speak your name aloud)

—you are a Light-Bearer.

Deep in the sanctuary of your heart you carry the Light of God. Yours it is bring that forth to light the path of those walking through life with you.

Yours it is to light their way out of confusion, personal darkness and despair.

Let your light shine right where you are in your life's situations and circumstances—right where you are in that seemingly unimportant backwater place; right where you are in that seemingly menial position.

What is your Light? It is your smile and your laughter. It is your genuine concern for another in need.

It is your compassion and your courage. It is your intuitive understanding of what is needed in the moment.

It is your spiritual strength that sustains and empowers others on their arduous journey.

All of these are your Light—begotten of God.

Close your eyes in meditation now and contemplate the meaning of these words for yourself:

I am the light of the world.
I have the courage to let my light shine
everywhere I go today.

TODAY, I AM GRATEFUL FOR: _____

_____

GOD'S DAY 11 — *Uniqueness*

Remember, _____,
(speak your name aloud)

—you are unique,
you are special!

In creation there are no duplicates, no carbon copies, for each of us is a priceless original!

Just as each snowflake is a one-of-a-kind creation of a basic hexagonal pattern, so each individual is unique, yet expresses the original pattern the Creator intended. Give thanks for the unique expression of Life that *you* are!

God created someone of great worth when you were created, so don't try to be an imitation of anyone else.

Be yourself—your *Best Self*!

In your prayer today, love and honor your own uniqueness, as you honor and love the uniqueness of others!

Today I honor my divine uniqueness.
Today I honor my unique talents and abilities.
Today I know that I am unique and worth loving.
Thank You, God!

*TODAY, I AM GRATEFUL FOR:*_____

GOD'S DAY 12 — *Right Thinking*

Remember, _____,
  (speak your name aloud)

—you are the landlord of your house of consciousness.
Give an eviction notice to all those thoughts and feelings
that you do not want living there.

Just as a landlord screens people desiring to rent in his building to make sure they will not harm it but will be good tenants, so you must screen any thoughts and feelings coming into your house of consciousness.

If you find a troublesome thought or belief already in residence, be the decisive landlord and evict that unwanted tenant immediately!

Visualize opening the door of your mind and filling it with light, love, peace, and joy.

In your quiet time now, meditate on these words:

I am the landlord of my house of consciousness.
I give an eviction notice to all that I do not want living there.
I now invite God's thoughts of life, love, and peace
to take up residence in my house of consciousness.

TODAY, I AM GRATEFUL FOR: _____

_____

GOD'S DAY 13 — I AM

Remember, _____,
              (speak your name aloud)

                —to simply BE today!

Let go of doing.

Let go, for just a moment, of the roles that society has placed upon you—breadwinner, responsible parent, caregiver, spouse, career person, and the hundred other roles that weigh you down and make you conform.

In your quiet time now, close your eyes, take a deep breath, and let go of those roles and simply settle into a neutral zone, a peaceful state of mind.

                Peace...be still.

Meditate on *I AM*—the sacred name of God as revealed to Moses in his mystical "burning bush" experience in his inner dialogue with God.

Breathe in on *I*.

Out on AM

Not *I AM* this, or *I AM* that, but simply *I...AM*.

Rest in that *I Am-ness*, that Presence. Feel it restore your spirit. Feel it calm your mind.

Be one with that love, that peace. Be.

*TODAY, I AM GRATEFUL FOR:*_____

_____

GOD'S DAY 14 — Surrender

Remember, _____,
        (speak your name aloud)

*—to drop the veil of the ego that separates you
from the awareness of God's presence within you.*

In the ancient temple of Jerusalem a veil separated the inner court of worship from the Holy of Holies, where the high priest was permitted to enter but once a year, and then only after he had performed acts of fasting and self- purification.

Likewise, you cannot enter into the Holy of Holies in the inner temple of your soul until you first totally surrender your personal ego with its ignorance and fear.

You cannot enter the Secret Place of the Most High— that place of Infinite Peace, Love, and Joy unless you first cleanse your heart of its fear, its resentments, its lusts and its loneliness.

In your quiet time today, seek the Secret Place.

*Loving Lord of my being. Here is my heart.
Cleanse it of its fears, and self-doubts, its resentments,
its lusts and its loneliness.
I surrender myself, my entire being to You.
Admit me into Your Holy of Holies
that I may be one with You,
Your Love, Your Peace, and Your Joy.*

TODAY, I AM GRATEFUL FOR: _____

_____

GOD'S DAY 15 — *Holy Moments*

Remember, _____,
> (speak your name aloud)

> *—there are holy moments awaiting you today.*

Moments of awe when you see a scene of incredible beauty in a commonplace city street.

Moments when you see the touch of God's grace in a common face—a spark of the Divine shining through the eyes of a supermarket checker, or in the eyes of an aged person huddled in a wheelchair.

Be grateful.

God has just blessed you with a holy moment of awe.

Open yourself to be a holy moment of awe for someone else today.

Let your prayer be:

> *Today, Lord, make me aware*
> *of the moments of awe You have for me.*
> *Make me an agent of Your grace.*

*TODAY, I AM GRATEFUL FOR:*_____

_____

GOD'S DAY 16 — *Anticipate the Best*

Remember,_____,
(speak your name aloud)

—you have two choices today—

You can look ahead with dread
or
you can anticipate the best with zest!

Like focusing binoculars to look beyond the foreground to a distant scene, you can look beyond the dread to the best.

Ask yourself:

Have I been 'looking ahead with dread"—fearing a worst-case scenario—or have I been trusting in God to bring about the best?

The best is waiting there for you. It only requires that you re-focus your eyes to the Goodness that God has prepared for you just beyond the outer appearances that you dread.

Meditate on these words and anticipate God's Best:

I trust in God to bring Good from this situation for me.
I look beyond the appearances and
I anticipate God's Best with zest!
Thank you, God!

TODAY, I AM GRATEFUL FOR: _____

_____

GOD'S DAY 17 — Right Place

Remember, _____,
(speak your name aloud)

*—if indeed, your soul knows more about what is going on
than you can consciously know, then you are always
where you are supposed to be.*

You are always in your right place to experience what you need to experience for your soul's growth.

So whatever is going on in your life at present, it is an opportunity for you to learn to overcome and awaken to the Power of God within you.

Knowing this you can take a higher perspective of your situation. You can seek the higher good in it. You can stop bemoaning your situation and place yourself in God's wise and loving care.

Let your prayer be:

*Beloved Lord, show me how to extract the blessing
from this experience.
Open my eyes to the Truth.
Give me the perspective to see the higher purpose
that this experience is serving.*

*TODAY, I AM GRATEFUL FOR:*_____

_____

GOD'S DAY 18 — Higher Purpose

Remember, _____,
             (speak your name aloud)

—your body was meant to be an instrument to express
God's love, joy, and creativity.
It is a temple of the spirit of the living God.

It was created to sing and dance, to work in joy, and gaze at sunrises and sunsets, and play and make love.

It was created to heal and comfort, to embrace, and to lend a helping hand. It was created to bring beautiful places and magnificent palaces into being.

It is a precious instrument endowed by its Creator with awesome talents and powers sublime.

It is up to you to use it for the purposes for which it was originally created.

Today give thanks for it. Bless it, and be grateful for it, and invite God to use it for higher purposes.

Let your prayer be:

Here I am, Lord, use me!

TODAY, I AM GRATEFUL FOR: _____

_____

GOD'S DAY 19 — *God's Love*

Remember, _____,
(speak your name aloud)

*—you are the fire others
warm themselves by.*

The Fire of God's Infinite Love glows in your heart. From that warm hearth let that Love radiate forth to bless others.

The world needs your love to warm itself by—to heal itself by.

Meditate now on that Holy Fire in the fireplace of your heart. Feel God's Love warming you and radiating through your entire body and energy field.

Let your prayer be:

*The Fire of God's Infinite Love burns in my heart.
I am aglow with the sacred Fire of Life, Love, and Peace.
I extend that Fire to my world
as compassion to heal the broken-hearted,
as comfort for those grieving and without hope,
as gentleness to heal the wounded.*

*TODAY, I AM GRATEFUL FOR:*_____

_____

GOD'S DAY 20 — *Confidence*

Remember, _____,
> (speak your name aloud)

> *—the greatest mistake you can make in life,*
> *is to be continually fearing you will make one!*

In truth, there are no mistakes, for what is called a mistake is simply an opportunity to learn, to grow, to find your best means of expression. And so, the only mistake is living timidly —fearful of making a mistake.

Right now, agree to express your dauntless spirit! Agree to have a fearless attitude as you approach your assignments and challenges.

Step out boldly as the confident person that you truly are, and surprise even yourself!

In your meditation now see yourself as confident and faith-filled. See yourself boldly moving forward to accomplish that which you have been afraid to begin.

Declare:

> *With God as my guide,*
> *I move forward with courage and confidence!*
> *With God as my guide,*
> *I live life boldly and fearlessly!*

TODAY, I AM GRATEFUL FOR: _____

_____

GOD'S DAY 21 — Love

Remember, _____,

(speak your name aloud)

—that love fulfills the Law—

—the Law of Cause and Effect, of Sowing and Reaping, of karmic comeback.

Love is lord over karma.

Let love set your karma in motion to return a blessing to you.

Let compassion and goodwill go forth to meet your day.

In your quiet time now, close your eyes and hold this thought:

*I send the spirit of Divine Love before me this day
to make joyous and successful my way.
It goes before me to greet me at every step of my way.
It goes before me to bless every person I meet today.*

*TODAY, I AM GRATEFUL FOR:*_____

_____

GOD'S DAY 22 — *Self-Renewal*

Remember, _____,
              (speak your name aloud)

        —to take a day for yourself.

Let your soul catch up with your body racing with the busy-ness of the world.

Get out for a walk. Walk the stress away.

Read one of those books you haven't had time to read. Play some of your favorite music.

Start a creative project that will feed your soul.

Sign up for a spiritual retreat or workshop.

By the end of the day you will feel refreshed and renewed. The vague anxiety will have evaporated, and you will feel that your soul is once again in touch with your higher Self.

Today, take time to nourish your soul!

TODAY, I AM GRATEFUL FOR: _____

_____

GOD'S DAY 23 — *Clear Channel*

Remember, _____,
                 (speak your name aloud)

—to get yourself out of the way today, so that Spirit can express through you, think through you, and love through you.

This is your purpose—to be a clear channel for your True Self to live through, and work through.

Of yourself you can do nothing of lasting value anyway. It is only your little ego mind that thinks it is doing everything.

Simply become an instrument. That is your one function. As you allow your Higher Self to work through you, gone will be the worries and responsibilities of life. They are no longer yours.

Relax now in your meditation, and invite your Higher Power to work through you today.

Let your prayer be:

Loving Lord, here I am—live through me,
think through me, and love through me today.

Direct me in the paths you would have me go.
Direct me to the people you would have me meet today.
I am yours to direct.

TODAY, I AM GRATEFUL FOR:_____

_____

GOD'S DAY 24 — *Right Choice*

Remember, _____,
        (speak your name aloud)

> *—the world can get along very well*
> *without your worries and complaints,*
> *—but it does need you to be a blessing.*

It does need you to lift the spirits of those who are discouraged.

It does need your laughter, and your light-hearted touch.

You can be a blessing or a burden today,

which will it be?

Your life, your world, and the people in your world are waiting for you to make your choice.

Declare:

> *Today, I choose happiness, not gloom.*
> *Today I choose laughter instead of sadness.*
> *Today, I choose_____.*

TODAY, I AM GRATEFUL FOR: _____

_____

GOD'S DAY 25 — *Happiness*

Remember, _____,
(speak your name aloud)

*—if you are depending on another person
for your happiness you are giving away your power
to be happy.*

Unless you tap the Source of happiness within yourself, true happiness will elude you. Expecting others to make you happy won't work—that is your own responsibility.

Neither are you responsible for making others happy. That is their responsibility.

You may see a family member making choices that are not for his or her highest good. You may feel like rushing in and rescuing them, but if you do, you may actually be enabling them in their weakness, or smothering them—with the result that no one is happy!

Stand ready to help if help should be requested, but do not force your wishes upon them.

What you can do now is reach out and lift their spirit in prayer. In your meditation visualize the Presence of the Christ within their heart. Place them in the care of that Spirit of unconditional love and wisdom within them.

Pray:

*Trusting and Resting, I release you into the care
of the Christ to guide, protect and provide for you.*

TODAY, I AM GRATEFUL FOR:_____

GOD'S DAY 26 — *Highest Prayer*

Remember, _____,
              (speak your name aloud)

*—your thoughts are prayers, and you are constantly praying
because your mind never stops thinking.*

The downside is that some prayers are negative, because
that is where your thoughts are at that moment, and you
wouldn't want those prayers to be answered!

Your highest prayers are prayed from the highest point of
view— knowing that God is the only Reality of us, beyond our
outer appearances.

The *Transcendent Treatment Prayer* by H.B. Jeffery,
speaks to the higher nature in the person you are praying for.

Here it is in excerpted form. Use it in your prayer time now.

Beloved of God—greeting!
In my integrity within me, where I know and see as God,
I know and see you, O beloved, to be free, wise, and immortal!
I see you unfettered and unbound,
triumphant! glorious! splendid!
. . . see you unbound, undiseased, buoyant!
I see you strong! mighty! forceful! powerful! divine!
. . . I behold you bright! joyous!
I see you victorious! undaunted!
I see you spotless! beautiful!
I see you flawless! fearless!
Transcending yourself and all your affairs—independent!
I see you smiling! sound! sane! strong!
. . . I see you alive with God
and upheld by His free Spirit forever! [2]

TODAY, I AM GRATEFUL FOR: _____

_____

GOD'S DAY 27 — Fly-By Blessings

Remember, _____,

(speak your name aloud)

—to claim the blessings that come your way today.

There are fly-by blessings all around you—be conscious of them!

That little boy grinning at you impishly in the supermarket.

Your fellow worker who thought to bring you a cup of coffee.

The driver of the car on the busy street, holding back for you to slip into traffic—did you catch those blessings?

This very moment has a blessing waiting for you to claim it by saying *Thank You!*

Take a quiet moment now, to say *Thank You* for the fly-by blessings that already have come to you today.

TODAY, I AM GRATEFUL FOR: _____

_____

GOD'S DAY 28 — *All-Sufficiency*

Remember, _____,
          (speak your name aloud)

> —*God is the Source of your Supply,*
> *your All-Sufficiency on every level of your Being.*

When you are doing your bills and writing checks, do you find yourself thinking or saying:

"There won't be enough money for this or that,"

"Where will the money come from?"

Those words betray you, for they show that you are not really trusting in the Source of all your Good.

The next time you are experiencing seemingly hard times financially, use that time to hold to the truth that God truly is your All-Sufficiency in all things!

In your quiet time today, meditate on these truths:

> *God is the Source of my Supply—*
> *my All-Sufficiency on every level of my Being.*

> *Right now, this very moment, this very hour,*
> *my every need is met with the right supply,*
> *and I am grateful!*

> *Know this truth, and see your Good coming forth!*
> *God is blessing you right now, with abundance!*

TODAY, I AM GRATEFUL FOR: _____
_____

GOD'S DAY 29 — *Seeing Clearly*

Remember, _____,
           (speak your name aloud)

—you are not living with people,
you are living with your concept of them.

The world you live in is first of all the world of concepts that you have created with your own thoughts and attitudes. It is your own unique construct.

If you are seeing through the clouded cataracts of your old fears and distorted beliefs, the world is an unfriendly place.

On the other hand, if you believe the universe is friendly, then you will experience a world filled with people of goodwill who respect and support each other.

Today, take a look at the people in your life.

Realize that you see and judge them by *what is in you.* For as you see them, so you see yourself. So accept them as they really are—sons and daughters of Life—at various stages of awareness and unfoldment.

Erase any distorted concepts you may be holding of them, and begin to see people with new eyes —eyes of love!

Hold this thought:

Loving Presence, help me to see clearly with eyes of love.
Help me to remove the cataracts of fear and judgment from
my inner eye and see your beauty and goodness
in everyone I meet today.

TODAY, I AM GRATEFUL FOR:_____

GOD'S DAY 30 — *Day-Tight Compartments*

Remember, _____,
      (speak your name aloud)

*—to live each day in a "day-tight"
    compartment!*

On great ocean liners, the hold of the ship is partitioned into a series of bulkheads and doors that can be sealed off to prevent seawater from flooding the entire ship in case of an accident that damages the hull. The water is confined to one compartment, keeping the ship safe and afloat.

Do not let tomorrow's worries flood the present moment.

Arrange your day in "day-tight' compartments. Live one day, one hour at a time. Keep your mind focused on the moment and work at hand.

Keep your energy and attention confined to one-hour compartments. Pull your wandering mind back to the task at hand by saying, *"Right here, Right now_____"*

Hold to this thought:

> *Right now, this very moment, this very hour,*
> *I focus on the work at hand.*
> *Thank you, God!*

TODAY, I AM GRATEFUL FOR: _____

_____

GOD'S DAY 31 — God's Butterflies

Remember, _____
> (speak your name aloud)

> *—why walk when you can fly!*

The intellect plods, but intuitive ideas fly!

Use both sides of your mind—your heart's wisdom, as well as your everyday conventional intellect.

Get your net and catch those intuitive butterflies! Aren't they beautiful!

Whoops! There goes one now—just the beautiful answer you need to your problem, too! What a shame you missed it— too busy trying to figure things out on your own.

God's butterflies are all around you, waiting to be caught.

Take a moment now, in your quiet time to listen.

Let your prayer be:

> *Lord, I open the net of my mind to you.*
> *Fill it with Your beautiful ideas..*
> *Fill my heart with Your Love.*
> *In quietness and peace I wait.*
> *Fill me with your Presence.*

*TODAY, I AM GRATEFUL FOR:*_____

_____

GOD'S DAY 32 — *Higher Self*

Remember, _____,

        (speak your name aloud)

        —you are not living this life.

It is your Higher Power that is living, loving and working through you to accomplish the higher plan for your soul'

You cannot move a finger without the Life and Strength of God that animates your body temple.

You cannot think a thought except by the Mind of God that is the parent of your conscious awareness.

Acknowledge that Source. Cling to it. Affirm it. Live from it, think from it, and act from it.

Relax and let your divine Self express and work through you.

Close your eyes and hold this thought:

        Divine Self, live this day through me.

        Make the decisions.

Work the work you would have done through me today.

TODAY, I AM GRATEFUL FOR: _____

_____

GOD'S DAY 33 — God in Expression

Remember, _____,
(speak your name aloud)

*—you are here to re-present God,
that is, to present again the Life, Love and Joy that God is!*

As the spiritual image and likeness of God, you are God in expression.

Put aside lesser goals and hold to this grand purpose of *re-presenting* the Life, Love and Joy of God to your world.

Let your prayer be:

*God be in my mind, and in my understanding.
Be in my eyes and in my seeing.
Be in my voice and in my speaking.
Be in my hands and in my doing.
Be in my feet and in all my comings and goings.
Take me where Your Life, Love and Joy need to be.
Use me for Your good purposes.*

Today, dedicate yourself to *re-presenting* God to your world!

*TODAY, I AM GRATEFUL FOR:*_____

_____

GOD'S DAY 34 — *Laughter*

Remember, _____,
> (speak your name aloud)

>> *—to loosen up and laugh!*

When was the last time you really laughed—laughed so hard that your whole being shook, and you could feel the old inner states of fear—of holding back, of procrastination—breaking up?

Do you remember rolling down a hill as a child—shouting and laughing with total abandon?

Would you dare to do that today if you had the opportunity? Or are you too straight-jacketed by your stuffy grownup propriety to try it?

Close you eyes for a moment. Imagine yourself as a child again, rolling down that grassy hill. Feel the rolling giddiness. See yourself laughing and free!

Today, loosen up and let go of your constraints. Let your inner child out to play, and let laughter ring out through your being!

TODAY, I AM GRATEFUL FOR: _____

_____

GOD'S DAY 35 — *Support Team*

Remember, _____,
          (speak your name aloud)

         —You are not facing life alone.

Do you know you have a support team of loved ones and angels in the spiritual dimension who are always with you, giving you their love and encouragement?

A band of angels, if you will, who are only a thought away. They walk beside you and guide your way. They are with you when you pray, multiplying God's power, and they are with you even when you forget to pray.

Call upon them when you are driving your car. Send them to surround someone who needs protection or healing.

Today, be aware of their presence, and know that you are never alone. Your spiritual support team is always with you.

In your quiet time now, thank each one for their love, their guidance, and protection.

*TODAY, I AM GRATEFUL FOR:*_____

_____

GOD'S DAY 36 — *Full Potential*

Remember, _____,
                (speak your name aloud)

           —*you are a changeling.*

You came into this world changing from a water-borne creature to an air-breathing infant—a radical metamorphosis—and you have been changing ever since.

You are a butterfly in caterpillar form, waiting to change into your full potential.

The urge to change in you is the Spirit of God in you, ever urging you to evolve into your full beauty and expression.

In your meditation now, pray:

Lord, change me at depth, that I may receive Your blessing
Change me into your spiritual image and likeness.

Change me into your expression of
infinite Love, and Peace, and Power.

Change me from lower to higher—
from a caterpillar mentality to a butterfly consciousness.
Lord, show me Your blessing in this change.

TODAY, I AM GRATEFUL FOR: _____

_____

GOD'S DAY 37 — Reclaim Your Power

Remember, _____,
(speak your name aloud)

—to ask yourself this question today:

*Who or what is holding me back
from what I truly desire to be or do?*

Take a moment now in meditation to scan your mind. See what person or situation pops up as standing in the way of your good. Jot down a list of whom or what you are blaming.

As you look at the list and you will find there is really only one person who is holding you back—yourself!

None of the other persons or circumstances on the list really has the power to prevent you from being your best except for the poveer you give to them by fearing, doubting, and resenting.

Your Higher Self stands patiently by waiting for you to re-claim your power. Step out on faith and take that first step to break free. Speak this truth to yourself, today:

*No person, situation or condition can keep me from my good,
and no person, situation or condition
can keep my good from me!
I am mightier than any circumstances.
Through the power of the Indwelling Christ within me,
I now forgive, release, and dissolve all blocks to my Good.
I move forward to the Good God has for me now!*

*TODAY, I AM GRATEFUL FOR:*_____

GOD'S DAY 38 — *Insight into Illness*

Remember, _____,
(speak your name aloud)

> *—there is a gift of insight and understanding*
> *hidden in every illness, if you are willing to receive it.*

Sometimes you are so busy fearing the illness or trying to heal it, you miss the message it brings from the deeper levels of your soul.

Remember your body is a "messenger," reporting what is going on not only in your physical self, but also in your soul, your emotions and outer life, as well. There is always a mind/body connection.

Do not slam the door in the messenger's face just because you don't like its "looks"(the appearance of the illness, or the negative feelings of the emotional distress).   ·

In your quiet time, dialogue with the condition. Ask the Lord to help you "talk" to the condition. First, bless the illness, and ask:

> *Illness, what is your message?*
> *What or who do you represent in my life?*
> *What are you trying to tell me on the soul level?*
> *What changes do I need to make?*
> *Who do I need to forgive?*

Follow through with forgiveness and make the changes indicated. As you accomplish this inner healing it clears the way for physical healing. Bless your body and release it into God's loving, healing care.

TODAY, I AM GRATEFUL FOR: _____

_____

GOD'S DAY 39 — Present Moment

Remember, _____,
            (speak your name aloud)

—you are a point of Light between two darknesses—
            the past and the future.

The past is dark and the future is unknown.

Only in this present moment can you break free of the chains of the past and the fears of the future, because only in the present moment can you access God's Wisdom and Power.

This is a powerful idea that will deliver you from the bondage of the past and the tyranny of the future.

Today, meditate on this statement and repeat it to yourself during the day:

Right now, this very moment is the moment of power.

Right now, this very moment I let go
of past darkness and doubt.

Right now, this very moment
I move forward in the light and love of God.

TODAY, I AM GRATEFUL FOR: _____

_____

GOD'S DAY 40 — *Compassion*

Remember, _____,
           (speak your name aloud)

   —to be compassionate, because we are all one.

Think not that there is a separation between you and the rest of humanity. You are inseparably connected on the soul level.

If those you consider to be your enemy suffer a misfortune, it is also your misfortune. If they lie dying, a part of you lies dying also. There is no "you and them," there is only us. "Send not to ask for whom the bell tolls, it tolls for thee."

To be compassionate does not mean to be a doormat for others to step on. It means to function from a higher consciousness knowing that we are all connected on the soul level, and that which blesses one blesses all.

We are all in the same lifeboat adrift on the sea of Earthly experience.

In your quiet time now, center your attention in your heart, and from that center of God's Love send forth an energy wave of compassion to encircle those you may have been judging or condemning.

See it dissolving all inharmony.

See that love filling their hearts and healing them.

TODAY, I AM GRATEFUL FOR: _____

_____

GOD'S DAY 41 — *Choice*

Remember, _____,
    (speak your name aloud)

—there are only two states of mind—Love and Fear.
One gives life, and the other destroys.

Which will you choose today?

Will you choose a consciousness of love and compassion to strengthen your immune system, or a consciousness of fear and anxiety that weakens it?

Which will you choose today?

As you know deeply that you are a beloved child of God, you will build a consciousness of worthiness, and health of mind and body.

Remind yourself today:

I choose love!
I choose life!
I choose to trust
in the one Power and Presence—
ever-sustaining and ever-providing for me today!

*TODAY, I AM GRATEFUL FOR:*_____

GOD'S DAY 42 — *Power of Love*

Remember, _____,
(speak your name aloud)

—*true love gives.*

Love does not ask, "Is this person worthy of my love?"

It shares freely, as needed, without reservation.

True love *frees.* It never possesses another, but acknowledges every person's divine right to be free.

True love *cares.* It is the feeling of genuine compassion that communicates to all, "I care about you and what happens to you."

True love *endures!* It does not come and go, but is steady, constant, eternal.

True love is the love of God in everyone of us and it's ours to *share.*

Today, find a way to express unconditional love to someone!

Let your prayer be:

Lord, show me a way
to share your love with someone today.

TODAY, I AM GRATEFUL FOR: _____

_____

GOD'S DAY 43 — All In Good Time

Remember, _____,
          (speak your name aloud)

—"later" is a very important word.

Have you ever noticed how worldly thoughts and duties muscle in to demand your attention just as you are about to pray or meditate?

Like a little child that tugs at his mother's sleeve, saying, "Me first, Mommy!"

Be firm with those worldly thoughts tugging at your sleeve. Simply say to them: *Later, all in good time.*

If you say "No", they will resist and persist, but *"later"* pushes them quietly into the background so you can finish your meditation. If they pop in again, a second *"later"* will quiet those thoughts. Let them go.

Today in your meditation time, ignore the thoughts tugging at the sleeve of your mind, urging you to hurry, saying you do not have time to meditate.

Say *"later"* to them and continue communing with the Source of your strength, peace and power. Charge your soul with that divine energy, then peacefully go about your daily activities.

Once you have taken care of nourishing your soul first, you will find you have all the time you need to take care of what needs to be done.

TODAY, I AM GRATEFUL FOR: _____

GOD'S DAY 44 — *Command*

Remember, _____,
    (speak your name aloud)

—today is waiting for you to name what it shall be.

Today will become whatever you name it to be—
joyous or sad, filled with serendipity or bad.

Take command of it now.

Name it and declare it to be!

In your meditation fill in the blanks:

I declare this day to be_____

I declare this day to be_____

I declare this day to be_____

I declare this day to be_____

    Thank you, Spirit, it is so!

TODAY, I AM GRATEFUL FOR: _____

_____

GOD'S DAY 45 — *Surrender*

Remember, _____,
  (speak your name aloud)

  —in every difficulty, whether you are aware of it or not,
    your Higher Self is calling to you, saying:
    "Look unto me, come to me, give it to me.
    I will take care of it for you."

People in the 12-step recovery programs often say that the best thing that ever happened to them was to hit bottom in their addiction, because that is when they surrendered and found their Higher Power.

Why wait to hit bottom with your problem when you can turn within to that Higher Power right now.

Let your prayer be:

  Thank you, Higher Power that you are always within me,
    guiding and strengthening me.
    I turn myself over to Your care today.
    Take over!

*TODAY, I AM GRATEFUL FOR:*_____

GOD'S DAY 46 — Strength

Remember, _____,
             (speak your name aloud)

—when you are feeling stressed-out and in need of more strength and vitality, speak these words to yourself:

I am strong in the Lord,
and in the power of his might.

Repeat them to overcome feelings of weakness, or symptoms of illness.

Use them when you need courage to face a difficult situation.

Speak them in your prayers for others.

You are strong in the Lord,
and in the power of his might.

In your quiet time now, hold that thought strongly. Let it reconnect you with God's power, strength, and vitality.

I am strong in the Lord,
and in the power of his might.

TODAY, I AM GRATEFUL FOR: _____

_____

Stronger than your fears

I am that in you
that is stronger than your fears.
I am that in you that knows the way through
— I am the Knower.
I am that in you that watches over you
whenever you feel alone and afraid.

I go with you wherever you go—I am the Watcher.
I am that in you that overcomes—I am the Overcomer.
I am that in you that sees beyond the darkness
to the shining path ahead—I am the Seer.
I am that in you that rejoices at victory.
I am that in you that Provides when all else fails...
Come unto me.

I am that in you that is eternal—untouched by years.
I am the very Breath of Life in you.
You live and move and have your Being in Me.
I am the Christ.
Let Me be Me in you,
until the illusion of separateness is dissolved,
and we are One.
I am the Strength you seek.
I am the Love you yearn for.
Come unto me.
I am the Christ.

...the mystery hidden for ages...which is Christ in you...
(Col.1:26-27)
The Kingdom of God is within you...
(Luke 17:21)
Lo, I am with you always...
(Matt. 28:20)

GOD'S DAY 47 — Awaken

Remember, _____,
　　　　　　(speak your name aloud)
　　　　—you have chosen to be here.

You have chosen to come here from the realm of Light—to be a bringer of Christ Truth and Love to your world.

You have chosen to create this body form; to animate it with your spirit, and inhabit it. You are its creator. At the highest level of your soul, you have the power to heal it, as well as to lay it aside as you choose.

Your soul has chosen the scenarios that would best serve your soul's purposes. But remember, you are more than these. You are not to be a victim of them. You are only participating in them as an actor plays a role, but you are more that role.

You have forgotten why you have come, and are lost in the clouds of unknowing. But you are awakening now to your true purpose as a bearer of Light and Love.

Close your outer eyes now, and open your inner eyes to behold the splendor of your true being.

Visit the Upper Room of Light and rest there before the altar. Ask your Indwelling Christ who waits there for you—to awaken you, to help you to remember, and to re-direct you on your life's path.

Lord, awaken me. Help me to remember.
Re-direct me onto my true path.

TODAY, I AM GRATEFUL FOR: _____

_____

GOD'S DAY 48 — *Breathing Break*

Remember, _____,
> (speak your name aloud)

> —*the power of a deep breath.*

During the day, when you are feeling pressured and your mind is racing, take a Breathing Break.

Pull your mind away from the fretting.

Breathe in on *Peace.*

Breathe out on *I let go and let God take charge.*

In that moment of deep breathing and release, your mind will clear of stress and open to the strengthening power of God.

New vitality and new solutions will flow into you on the carrier wave of your breath.

Right now, consciously take a deep slow breath, as you say:

> *Peace, Be Still.*
> *I breathe in God's Peace,*
> *I breathe out doubt and hurry.*
> *I breathe in God's Peace,*
> *and I let the power of God take charge.*

*TODAY, I AM GRATEFUL FOR:*_____

GOD'S DAY 49 — Be the Observer

Remember, _____,
(speak your name aloud)

> *—to break out of your daytime dream state*
> *Stop running on automatic.*

Be in the moment today, consciously aware of yourself and your surroundings.

Turn off the automatic pilot and take manual control of your thoughts and your feelings.

Be the conscious Observer, the conscious commander of your will.

Today make the moment-by-moment choice to listen to your Higher Guidance—the wisdom of your Higher Self.

In this consciously alert state you can take advantage of the opportunities that Spirit has placed in your path today.

In your quiet time now, hold this thought:

Today, I am consciously aware and alert to God's blessings.

I am consciously aware of my connection
with the One Source of All Good, All Love, all Supply.
And I am grateful!

TODAY, I AM GRATEFUL FOR: _____

_____

GOD'S DAY 50 — Reach Out

Remember, _____,
(speak your name aloud)

—to reach out to others today.

If you discovered that you only had five minutes left in life to say all you wanted to say to the people in your life, you would be telephoning them to stammer that you loved them.

It is always later than you think, but you have all the time you need. Seize this opportunity to reach out to another person right now.

Think of all the people you feel close to—the people you really love. How many times in the last year have you told those people that you loved them? Too few times, if at all.

Begin right now to express that love.

Make that call. Send that e-mail, that note.

It is not to late to tell someone you really care!

*TODAY, I AM GRATEFUL FOR:*_____

_____

GOD'S DAY 51 — Practice The Presence

Remember, _____,
> (speak your name aloud)

> —*your highest purpose on Earth is to P.T.P.—*
> *to practice the presence of God in your daily life.*

Practice being aware of God's Life animating your body.

Practice being aware of God's thoughts in your mind.

Practice being aware of God's Love and protection all around you. Practice seeing the goodness of God in everyone you meet.

As you practice living and working from your higher nature, you join ranks with others worldwide to form a critical mass to shift humanity to its next level of spiritual development.

You help humanity in its struggle to lift itself out of the morass of ignorance and materialism.

In your meditation today, ask your Higher Self to live, work, and love through you.

Let your prayer be:

> *Here I am, Lord,*
> *Live through me, work through me,*
> *and love through me.*
> *Let me be an instrument*
> *to accomplish your purposes today.*

TODAY, I AM GRATEFUL FOR: _____

GOD'S DAY 52 — Rest In God

Remember, _____,

        (speak your name aloud)

   —to let your mind return to the heart and remain there.

Bring all your wandering thoughts back home to the heart—the abode of God's Love within you and remain there.

In your meditation now, focus your attention on your breathing, relaxed and regular. Let the beating of your heart say over and over—

rest in love . . . rest in love . . . rest in love.

When the mind tries to slip away and wander out again, bring it back to lie still in that Secret Place of the Most High, until you merge with the peace of God that passes all understanding.

Peace...be still.
Rest . . . in God's love.

TODAY, I AM GRATEFUL FOR: _____

_____

GOD'S DAY 53 — *Power to Change*

Remember, _____,
> (speak your name aloud)

—you have the power to choose your thoughts,
and the power to choose your thoughts is the power
to change your life.

Remember, every mental image, every thought held in mind, is the engine of change. It is the seed of a new harvest of consequences.

What consequences do you want to set into motion today? What are you choosing for yourself today?

Set your intention with the following statements:

Today, I choose to be_____

Today, I choose to have_____

Today, I choose to feel_____

Today, I choose to think_____

Today, I choose to love_____

Today, I choose to act_____

TODAY, I AM GRATEFUL FOR: _____

_____

GOD'S DAY 54 — Transmitter of God's Love

Remember, _____,
(speak your name aloud)

*—love is what you are here for,
both to give and receive.*

Your only purpose is to be a transmitter of God's Love and Light.

Your happiness is entirely dependent on your ability to transmit love and beauty and pass it on.

If you are not happy, you are not doing your job.

Stop your complaining and start asking God to broadcast love through you today, laugh through you today, and create through you today.

Let your prayer be:

Lord, make me be a transmitter of Your love today.

TODAY, I AM GRATEFUL FOR:_____

GOD'S DAY 55 — *Color Your Day Happy*

Remember, _____,
          (speak your name aloud)

          —you choose the moods that color your day.

You don't have to wallow in unhappy moods.

Stop right now. Examine how you feel. Do you want that mood to color this day for you? If not, then picture how you would like to feel and choose to feel that way right now!

The choice is yours. It's as simple as that! Exercise your power of choice!

Close your eyes for a moment now and think back to a particular situation or nature scene where you were happy and peaceful.

Visualize being there. Feel it until it becomes real to you. Breathe in the peace of that scene. You have created a new mood of happiness for yourself.

Color your day with that happiness!

TODAY, I AM GRATEFUL FOR: _____

_____

GOD'S DAY 56 — *Make Friends with Change*

Remember, _____,
  (speak your name aloud)

  —to make friends with change.

Every change—be it in your career, relationships, or personal life—presents you with two options.

You can either meet it with resentment and fear and thus fall victim to it, or you can meet it with faith and extract the good from it.

Even the unhappiest changes can strengthen your faith muscles and serve to help you grow spiritually as you struggle to find your way through.

In your quiet time now, ask God to show you how to find the blessing hidden in the change for you.

Let your prayer be:

Lord, show me the blessing in this change.
I welcome this change as a part
of my spiritual unfoldment.

It leads me to greater good.
I can hardly wait to see the blessing
in this change for me.

*TODAY, I AM GRATEFUL FOR:*_____

_____

GOD'S DAY 57 — *Holy Ground*

Remember, _____,
(speak your name aloud)

—you are standing on Holy Ground.

You stand on Holy Ground because God's Presence consecrates everywhere you stand. Wherever you are, God is.

Today, remember that wherever you are—at home, at work, in the supermarket, or in the ghetto—you are standing on Holy Ground, for the Presence of God's Power and Protection is always there for you.

Wherever you find yourself to be at this moment, silently remember:

I am standing on Holy Ground.
God is here.
I am safe, and all is well.

TODAY, I AM GRATEFUL FOR: _____

_____

GOD'S DAY 58 — *Subliminal Influence*

Remember, _____,
(speak your name aloud)

*—live in a palace and you'll
think like a king,
live in poverty and you'll
think like a pauper.*

And it works the other way around too. Think like a king and you will live like a king, think like a pauper and you will live like a pauper.

In your quiet time now, scan your home—the pictures on the walls, the furnishings. Ask yourself if you really want them in your consciousness. Do they make you think like a king, or a pauper?

Do they add to the beauty of your soul? Make a mental note to discard anything that impacts your consciousness in a negative way.

Do the same at your place of work. Make the changes you need to create beauty.

It may be something as simple as adding a beautiful mural of a nature scene, or bringing in flowering plant. Whatever it is, it will nourish your spirit.

*TODAY, I AM GRATEFUL FOR:*_____

GOD'S DAY 59 — *Live in the Now*

Remember, _____,

(speak your name aloud)

—to make today count!

A man with terminal illness was given six months to live. When the family heard the doctor's prognosis they sank into despair. Joy faded from their home.

After a month of despair the man suddenly realized, "I'm not dead yet. Why not make today count!"

He said: "You know, its like being on a train, and far ahead of you down the track you see your final destination. But there are many station stops in-between. Instead of concentrating on that final destination, I decided to take advantage of each stop along the way and make the most of the remainder of the journey."

He became so excited with this idea of *making today count* that he launched into a program of helping other people face their so-called terminal illnesses—to live each day to its fullest and not to dwell upon what might happen.

That man lived several years beyond his six months prognosis. He took his mind off his fear of what might happen and began to live each day fully, in loving service.

As a result, he was blessed with length of days.

Make today count—live in the Now, for that's the only time you really have.

TODAY, I AM GRATEFUL FOR: _____

_____

GOD'S DAY 60 — Evildoers

Remember, _____,
                  (speak your name aloud)

—fret not over evildoers.

They will reap the rewards of their own karma. Don't get involved in their karma by judging or hating them, for you are only setting in motion a karmic comeback upon yourself.

Change the energy charge of your mental and emotional power from negative to positive by blessing and releasing these people to God. In this way you protect yourself from them and neutralize their energy.

In your quiet time now, bless and release them. Look beyond their outer faults to the Presence of God lying latent within them. Ask God to bless them and bring forth their better nature.

Let your prayer be:

Loving Spirit, help me to let go of my judgments.
Help me to see beyond their adverse appearances and actions
to your shining Presence at the core of their soul.

TODAY, I AM GRATEFUL FOR: _____

_____

GOD'S DAY 61 — *True Self*

Remember, _____,
(speak your name aloud)

—you are more than what you see in the mirror.

The person in the mirror is only the outer of you— the limited one that society and circumstances reflects back to you.

You are not seeing your True Self—the individual expression of the One, infinitely capable, and worthy.

If you look deeply into those eyes looking back at you in the mirror, you may catch a glimpse of Someone so powerful you will catch your breath in awe.

Angela Morgan describes this Someone in her poem "Know Thyself."

> *"...Fear not the goad, fear not the race,*
> *Plead not to fall from out the race—*
> *It is your Self driving you,*
> *Your Self that you have never known,*
> *Seeing your little self alone.*
> *Your Self, high-seated charioteer,*
> *Master of cowardice and fear,*
> *Your Self that sees the shining length*
> *Of all the fearful road ahead,*
> *Knows the terrors that you dread*
> *Are pigmies to your splendid strength;*
> *...Your Self that holds the mastering rein,*
> *Seeing beyond the sweat and pain*
> *And anguish of your driven soul,*
> *The patient beauty of the goal!"* [3]

Today, let this True Self empower you!

TODAY, I AM GRATEFUL FOR: _____

GOD'S DAY 62 — *Linked Together*

Remember, _____,
(speak your name aloud)

—all humanity is linked together
in one great broadcasting network,
spirit to spirit and soul to soul.

Your thoughts and actions are continuously broadcast and received over this vast telepathy energy grid.

As you use Truth to overcome your own challenges, you are also helping your brothers and sisters in the human family as well! Your breakthrough in consciousness makes it easier for everyone else on Earth to also make their own breakthrough.

Perhaps this is what Jesus meant when He said,

"And I, if I be lifted up will draw all men unto me."

Whenever we are lifted up in consciousness to the Power and Presence of God within us, we lift up countless others as well—just as their spiritual strength fortifies us in our times of need.

Today, be faithful to your part in lifting all of humanity.

Let your prayer be:

Lord, lift me with Your love
to see with higher understanding and compassion.
Let me beam Your love, light and peace to my world.

*TODAY, I AM GRATEFUL FOR:*_____

GOD'S DAY 63 — *Harmful Habits*

Remember, _____,
        (speak your name aloud)

        —to toss the dog a bone.

As you would distract a dog from chewing on your shoe by giving him a bone to chew on instead, so toss your mind an alternative "bone" to chew on when you feel the urge to indulge a harmful habit.

Defeat the habit by giving your mind an alternate image to focus on.

In your meditation now prepare that "bone" in advance by creating or finding a positive image of yourself engaged in an alternate constructive activity.

Today, remember to distract your mind with a positive bone!

TODAY, I AM GRATEFUL FOR: _____

_____

GOD'S DAY 64 — *Courage To Be Free*

Remember, _____,
     (speak your name aloud)

*—you are as free as you have the courage to deny power
to a situation or belief.*

Perhaps you feel someone in your family is pulling you down emotionally, or someone at work is causing you difficulty. Or you may believe that a certain condition in your personal life is blocking your way.

If that is what you believe, then that's the way it will be for you. Your are a prisoner of your own limited belief.

But if you boldly deny that anyone or any condition has the power to limit you then you are free. You have taken back your power.

Don't give your mental and emotional energy to limiting conditions and beliefs.

Today, boldly and strongly state:

You have no power to limit me!
You have no part in God's plan for my life!
Begone! I am free!

God is blessing you right now, with courage!

*TODAY, I AM GRATEFUL FOR:*_____

_____

GOD'S DAY 65 — *Let Go, Let God*

Remember, _____,
> (speak your name aloud)

> *—to detach from results.*

If you want peace of mind you must surrender the outcome of your desires to God.

—that cherished goal of yours? Surrender it to God's Love.

—that willful intent to make something happen—let it happen God's way.

—that "I-know-what's-best" for another person— surrender it to God and let God bring about the "best" for that person.

Let God's higher wisdom bring the best outworking for your highest good and the highest good of all concerned.

Let your prayer be:

> *Today, I let go, and let God take charge.*

TODAY, I AM GRATEFUL FOR: _____

GOD'S DAY 66 — *New Good*

Remember, _____,
           (speak your name aloud)

—to let go of missed opportunities and "might have beens."

If, while driving a car, you continually looked in the rear view mirror, you would drive into disaster!

This is true in life, also. If you are constantly looking back at what has been and what might have been, today's joy will whiz by you unnoticed.

Today, let go of what has been and be ready for the new good life has for you!

Let your prayer be:

Loving Spirit, I let go of the past, and I look forward
to the new good you have for me today!

*TODAY, I AM GRATEFUL FOR:*_____
_____

GOD'S DAY 67 — *Keep a Tight Rein*

Remember, _____,
> (speak your name aloud)

—to keep a tight rein on your imagination or it will run away with you, and like a runaway horse it will carry you headlong into disaster.

The imagination is a powerful horse that can be wild and headstrong. Ride it with a tight hand.

Remember the words of the apostle Paul:

"Casting down imaginations...and bringing into captivity every thought to the obedience of Christ."

Every image of personal disaster, every self-defeating thought must be brought under the obedience of Christ—that is, must be surrendered to the Indwelling Christ to be transformed.

In your quiet time now, pray:

Lord, take these unruly images and transform them with your peace, your power, and your love,

*TODAY, I AM GRATEFUL FOR:*_____

_____

GOD'S DAY 68 — *Eyes of Love.*

Remember, _____,

       (speak your name aloud)

       —only what is done in love will last!

All the rest fades away.

Take a moment to finish these sentences:

Today I love _____

Today I love being _____

Today I love having _____

Today I love experiencing _____

*Today I love giving*_____

*Today I love sharing*_____

*Today, I would love to*_____

Looking with eyes of love, you will find a whole new world around you.

And remember to look with eyes of love upon yourself as well, today!

TODAY, I AM GRATEFUL FOR: _____

_____

GOD'S DAY 69 — *The True You*

Remember, _____,
    (speak your name aloud)

*—beyond the clouds and confusion of your personal
consciousness is the pure, clear mind of God.*

In every cell of your body is the perfect Life of God, ever-renewing, ever-rebuilding and restoring your body according to that perfect pattern.

And beyond your false concept of yourself as a poor victim of circumstances, is the true You—strong, wise, capable and beautiful.

In meditation now, see yourself this way, and give thanks.

Close your eyes and see yourself shining and radiant.

*I am the Mind of God in expression—
pure, clear and wise.
I am the Radiant Life of God expressing
in a radiant energy form called the body.
Every atom and cell is animated by that Perfect Life now.
I am as God created me to be—strong, wise, capable and
beautiful.*

TODAY, I AM GRATEFUL FOR: _____

GOD'S DAY 70 — *One with the One*

Remember, _____,
        (speak your name aloud)

"I am as God is, and we are one."

That is the Truth about you.

You are as God is simply because God is really all there is—the Mind and Essence of all creation, formed and unformed.

You have no existence apart from God. Thus you partake of that divine nature. In your spiritual ignorance of this Truth, you may misuse that Energy, Life and Love that you derive from God—and create a hell of a life for yourself—but that does not change the truth about your basic, eternal nature.

Know this truth for yourself today, and draw upon that Creative Power within you for every desire and requirement. Trust and rest in that knowing.

In your quiet time now, meditate on this truth.

I am as God is, and we are one.

TODAY, I AM GRATEFUL FOR: _____

_____

GOD'S DAY 71 — *Your Mind, Your Servant*

Remember, _____,
            (speak your name aloud)

            —to take charge of your mind today!

Stop its negative chattering.

Direct it into positive channels. Your mind is supposed to be your servant, not your master. And its proper master is your Indwelling Christ. Place your mind under the direction of that Presence.

In your quiet time now, surrender your mind to that Master.

Let your prayer be:

Lord, here is my mind. I surrender it to You.
Cleanse it of its chatterings, its fears, and wallowings.
Think Your Divine Ideas through it.

Bless, love, and create through it according
to Your will and wisdom.

Fill it now with Your genius, Your joy, and Your peace.
Lord, here is my mind. I surrender it to You.

*TODAY, I AM GRATEFUL FOR:*_____
_____

GOD'S DAY 72 — *Start Anew Today*

Remember, _____,
(speak your name aloud)

—life is for living now!

Be happy now, not "I'll be happy when___."

Life is not to be postponed.

Consider what it is that you desire, right here, right now. You can at least be heading in the direction of your desires, and that knowledge will bring you present happiness.

Be the worker you would be even though conditions aren't perfect. As you adopt this attitude, you will find conditions changing and becoming as you wish them to be. Nothing in the outer can change until you first change within.

So postpone your life no longer. Be the person you desire to be and can be, right here, right now.

Hold this thought:

*Right now, this very moment, I make a new start
at living my life the way I desire it to be.*

*The universe is waiting for me
to make my commitment to happiness now!*

TODAY, I AM GRATEFUL FOR: _____
_____

GOD'S DAY 73 — *Self-forgiveness*

Remember, _____,
(speak your name aloud)

—to forgive yourself.

Until you are ready to forgive and release the past with all of those negative states of mind, you have locked yourself in a room filled with all the hurts, regrets, angers, and blames of your past.

The key of self-forgiveness is in your hands. Unlock the door and leave behind the room of horrors and despair. Escape into the sunshine of happiness.

In your quiet time now, invite God to help you forgive yourself and others, and ask forgiveness in return.

Pray:

Loving Lord, help me forgive myself.
Help me release my negative feelings toward others.
I now let go and fully forgive.

I now am free and fully forgiven.
I now let go and fully release.
Thank You, Lord. I am free!

*TODAY, I AM GRATEFUL FOR:*_____

_____

GOD'S DAY 74 — *Report To Headquarters*

Remember, _____,
(speak your name aloud)

—to start the day by reporting to "Headquarters."

Be like the military officer who began his day by praying, "*Reporting for duty, Sir. I await your orders.*"

Sit quietly now, and speak that prayer. Listen to the response from "Headquarters."

As you finish your prayer time, follow through on whatever silent instructions you receive about the business at hand. Your day will flow easily and in good order.

Write out and carry the following prayer in your pocket to re-center yourself during the pressures of the day:

*There is only One Power and One Presence in my life
and in the Universe— God, the Good, Omnipotent.*

*Right now, this very moment, this very hour,
God is setting things right and arranging my activities
for my Highest Good, and I am grateful.*

TODAY, I AM GRATEFUL FOR: _____

_____

GOD'S DAY 75 — Peace Awaits You

Remember, _____,
            (speak your name aloud)

—if you want peace you must bring all thoughts back to their point of rising—the I AM Presence of God within you.

In your quiet time now, observe your thoughts as they rise up in your mind. Follow each on back to its origin by asking of each one:

From where does this thought arise?

Who is thinking this thought?

This will shift your attention from the troublesome thoughts to concentrating on the source of the thought.

The answer will come:

Me, I am. I am thinking these thoughts.

Ask, *Who am I?*

The answer will come: *I AM. (the name of the presence and power of God within you.)*

Let your mind center and rest in that *I AM—*

in the Secret Place of the Most High within you.

Breathe in on *I.*

Breathe out on *AM.*

Be absorbed in it totally. Merge yourself with it until you feel at one with the Peace of God at the center of your being.

*TODAY, I AM GRATEFUL FOR:*_____

_____

GOD'S DAY 76 — *Power of Your Word*

Remember, _____,
　　　　　　(speak your name aloud)

　　　—every word you speak has your name on it.

　　Do you remember being in school when you wrote your name on your test papers? You knew those papers would come back to you, graded as to their quality.

　　So, too, our words return to us, graded according to the law of sowing and reaping. Our words are "seeds" which produce a harvest of like kind.

　　Every time we speak, we need to consider:

What am I sending forth?

Are my words kind?

Are they true?

Are they necessary?

Do they add to the greater good?

Today, remember this truth:

I am responsible for the words I speak.

—and then choose kind, positive, true words!

Pray:

　　Lord, let the words of my mouth and the meditations
　　　　of my heart be acceptable in Your sight.

TODAY, I AM GRATEFUL FOR: _____
_____

GOD'S DAY 77 — Sing Your Song

Remember, _____,
        (speak your name aloud)

—each of us has a song to sing—a song of creativity
that is uniquely ours.

Just as no two melodies are exactly alike, so our own song of creativity and the expression of our talents cannot be imitated.

We are not mockingbirds that imitate the songs of other birds. We came to sing our own song, and we will only be happy when we find a way to express it.

Today, let your creativity break forth and sing its song! Be the unique and beautiful you that you were created to be!

Keep this prayer statement taped to your mirror:

"No one and nothing can keep me from singing my Song—
the Song my Soul came to sing.

I sing it now and I rejoice!
Praise God!"

*TODAY, I AM GRATEFUL FOR:*_____

_____

GOD'S DAY 78 — *God's Protection*

Remember, _____,
                   (speak your name aloud)

*—to rise above the torrent of life upon
the wave of God's protection.*

As a surfer is lifted up by a great
wave and carried forward, so let the
wave of God's love and protection lift
you safely over the rushing waters of
life's crises.

Stay above the floodwaters of life's experiences by calling
upon the Power and Presence of God within you to lift and
support you.

Close your eyes now, and image yourself being lifted up by
a wave of God's Love and carried safely over your personal
crises.

TODAY, I AM GRATEFUL FOR: _____

_____

GOD'S DAY 79 — Spiritual Quest

Remember, _____,
         (speak your name aloud)

        —you have been here before.

You have watched in awe the glories of a sunrise.

You have heard the crashing of the waves upon distant beaches. You have walked the same paths that seem so vaguely familiar to you now.

And the persons in your life? Your soul has met their souls before on other journeys of self-discovery and in other classrooms of struggle and strife.

The crisis that faces you now—you have faced before. But this is the lifetime when you will overcome it once and for all. This is the lifetime you will understand the reason for it all.

This is the lifetime you are clearing up old fears, old mistakes, and this is the lifetime you are learning to forgive yourself and others, knowing you are all working through soul lessons together.

This is the lifetime when your prodigal soul awakens and returns to its loving Father.

Yes, you have been here before, in another guise, walking the path of the spiritual Quest, and this time you will find that which you have been questing. You will find it in the deep reaches of your own heart.

Be at peace. The Good Shepherd walks beside you on your Quest.

TODAY, I AM GRATEFUL FOR: _____

_____

GOD'S DAY 80 — *Mental Magnet*

Remember, _____,
(speak your name aloud)

*—your mind is a magnet,
and draws to you all of the experiences of your life.*

If you are not experiencing the good you desire or think you should have, change your mental magnet—your dominant thoughts and attitudes..

Get rid of the magnets of criticism, anger, bitterness, and grudges.

In their place think thoughts of goodwill, generosity, and helpfulness and these will attract the same to you.

In your meditation now, visualize a great magnet at your heart center—a magnet of God's Love, Peace, and Power. Visualize drawing to yourself your soul's sincerest desires.

*The magnet of God's Love deep in the heart of me
is now drawing to me the good I seek.
In deepest gratitude, I give thanks.*

TODAY, I AM GRATEFUL FOR: _____

GOD'S DAY 81 — Remember To Be

Remember, _____,
                (speak your name aloud)

          —doing is not being.

In all of your doing, take time to do a little being! Being is BE-ing. That is, being consciously aware of your true nature as an expression of God. Being consciously aware of God's Presence and Power at the center of your being.

Tune into that state of being now by taking a deep slow breath. Direct your attention into your heart, and feel the love, peace and power of God residing there in that sacred Inner Chamber.

As you breathe in, silently speak the words:

I am—

As you breathe out, silently say:

—one with God's Peace.

I am—one with God's peace.

After a few deep slow breaths you will feel refreshed and reconnected with your Source. Your day will go more smoothly and you will have more confidence and serenity in the midst of your daily tasks.

Today, remember to Be!

*TODAY, I AM GRATEFUL FOR:*_____
_____

GOD'S DAY 82 — *Trusting*

Remember, _____,
(speak your name aloud)

— to trust in God to open ways where to human sense there appears no way.

When you are faced with a sudden reversal in your finances or career, hold firm and trust that God is opening new and amazing channels to prosper and provide for you.

In the midst of your fears and doubts, know that new good is being prepared for you, in the right way and in the right time.

Make peace with the situation. Let go of any resentment and fear, and stay patient with an expectant attitude.

In your meditation, hold onto this thought:

I trust in God to open ways where to human sense there appears no way.

TODAY, I AM GRATEFUL FOR: _____
_____

GOD'S DAY 83 — Giving

Remember, _____,
(speak your name aloud)

—the great law of the universe says,
"Whatever you wish to receive, you first must give."

If you are feeling neglected, begin to pay attention to others and begin to appreciate them for what they are.

As you do so you will be surprised to find people beginning to notice and appreciate you!

Whatever it is that you need or desire in your life, begin by giving it away.

If you feel alone and without friends, ask:

'To whom can I be a friend today?"

And then be that friend. Reach out, make a phone call, or write a note.

Start giving of yourself today!
Start giving yourself away today!

*TODAY, I AM GRATEFUL FOR:*_____

_____

GOD'S DAY 84 — *Self-Realization*

Remember, _____,
        (speak your name aloud)

        —your only goal is Self-realization.
        What are you doing about it today?

You are here to bring your True Self into full expression. You are here to unfold and awaken to your divine qualities.

You are here to realize your true potential as a spiritual being—as an expression of God. And you are here to love—to be an instrument for Divine Love to heal the world.

What are you doing about it today?

Where and how are you going to express God's Love today?

To whom are you sending God's healing Light in your prayers?

Whom are you clothing in the protecting armor of God's Light to keep them safe?

        In your quiet moments now, answer these questions.

TODAY, I AM GRATEFUL FOR: _____

GOD'S DAY 85 — *Love Your Self*

Remember, _____,
(speak your name aloud)

—to take time for yourself today ... you are worth it!

You give time to everyone else, but you put yourself at the bottom of the list. There is no energy or time left over to love yourself.

More importantly, love your True Self—your higher nature.

Taking time for your Self is really taking time for the Spirit of God within you, which is often as neglected as your personal self and its needs.

Right now, this very moment, turn your attention into your heart and take a few silent breaths of gratitude and praise. Praise your human self, and praise your divine Self.

Let your meditation be:

"_____*(your name), I love you and praise you.*
I praise the Name of God within you.
I praise the radiant Life of God in your body temple.
I praise the Light of God's wisdom in your mind.
I praise the Love of God in your heart.

*TODAY, I AM GRATEFUL FOR:*_____

_____

GOD'S DAY 86 — Spiritual Teenager

Remember, _____,
(speak your name aloud)

> *—be patient with yourself.*
> *You are still a spiritual teenager.*

You are growing through the awkward stage of not knowing who you truly are—a spiritual being endowed with awesome powers of mind and spirit that you neither understand nor can control yet. Nor do you know that you are an object of your Beloved's affection.

You are like a sixteen-year-old behind the wheel of a Ferrari careening around the curves of life and sideswiping the guardrails.

Life is full of zits, and panic attacks, flashes of genius and fits of gloom.

And now the Beloved is asking you to dance!

That stunning, mysterious, awesome Beloved of your soul is saying to you: *"Dance with me!"*

And you stand there dumbstruck, with two left feet.

Awkward wallflower that you are, close your eyes and dance with the Beloved!

Lose your head and follow your heart!

> *Beloved, sweep me off my feet!*

TODAY, I AM GRATEFUL FOR: _____

_____

GOD'S DAY 87 — Guidance

Remember, _____,

(speak your name aloud)

—life is not a spreadsheet; don't make it one.

You cannot solve life's problems by analyzing the cold facts—spreadsheet style.

You only wind up with a wastebasket full of crumpled pro and con lists.

Go inside and ask your heart what it really desires.

Ask yourself:

What would make me the happiest?

Where do the people live that I am happiest to be near?

Where would I be happiest living?

What would I be happiest doing and being?

Then simply give it all up to God to handle.

Let your prayer be:

Lord, here is my life and affairs.
I place myself in your wise and loving care.
Lead me in the way of my good.
Thank You.
Amen

TODAY, I AM GRATEFUL FOR: _____

_____

GOD'S DAY 88 — *God's Will*

Remember, _____,
(speak your name aloud)

—the difficulties in your life can serve a higher purpose
of bringing you closer to God.

They are nudging you toward harmony with God's will.

When you find yourself in a frustrating or confusing situation, ask:

Spirit, what are you trying to tell me?
Where have I missed the mark?

As you listen, it may be obvious to you that you have forced your own will, instead of first checking out God's will for the situation.

Before every project, remember to take time to "tune into Spirit."

Breathe deeply to re-establish your conscious oneness with God. Ask what is to be accomplished through you in the activity you are about to begin, and then proceed as directed.

Take time now to tune into Spirit, before you begin your day.

Lord, re-align me to your loving will.

TODAY, I AM GRATEFUL FOR: _____

_____

GOD'S DAY 89 — Make a Difference

Remember, _____,

(speak your name aloud)

—you have the power to make a difference in someone's life.

Have you ever felt empowered by someone who believed in you and encouraged you—a family member, a neighbor, teacher, or friend—perhaps far back in childhood?

Take time right now to call him or her to mind and silently say:

"Thank you" to that person.

Who can you empower right now with an encouraging phone call, a note, or a helping hand?

It may be that at this very moment there is someone reaching out to you. No matter how small your action or prayer may seem, you are divinely appointed to be the right person at this very right time.

This moment is your Moment of Empowerment.

Do it today!

*TODAY, I AM GRATEFUL FOR:*_____

GOD'S DAY 90 — *Soul Growth*

Remember, _____,
(speak your name aloud)

—knotholes are for growing through!

Have you noticed that it is when you are feeling most pressured, most stretched to the limit, and squeezed breathless, that you make the greatest soul growth?

It is when your soul is being pulled through another knothole of fear or self-doubt, or resentment, that you grow the most.

Life is a crash course in learning to stop struggling and let God handle the crisis.

The degree of your discomfort, as you are pulled through the knotholes of your life, is determined by the degree of your resistance, or the degree of your willingness to grow through the experience.

Give it to God now in prayer, and ask to be shown the blessing in the experience.

Loving Spirit, I give this crisis into your hands.
Show me the blessing in it.

TODAY, I AM GRATEFUL FOR: _____

_____

GOD'S DAY 91 — *Inner Journey*

Remember, _____,
   (speak your name aloud)

—*to let your soul walk God's labyrinth today.*

At the center of the labyrinth is
the Peace of God that you seek.

In your quiet time close your eyes and picture yourself
entering the gate of the labyrinth—the outer entrance of your
mind.

Take a deep breath and release the cares and worries of the
day as you begin walking the winding path. Let it lead you
deeper into the quiet inner spaces. With the rhythm of each step
tell yourself— let . . . go, let . . . go, let . . . go.

Halfway in, your guardian angel waits to escort you into
the Secret Place at the center of the Labyrinth. There, in that
Sacred Space, surrender your problems, your ego, and merge
with the One.

Rest at the center until you are renewed in spirit, until you
once more remember your true identity as a spiritual child of the
Infinite.

Then begin your return journey, bringing out with you the
strength, peace, and wisdom garnered there.

*TODAY, I AM GRATEFUL FOR:*_____
_____

GOD'S DAY 92 — *Delays*

Remember, _____,
(speak your name aloud)

—*God's delays are not God's denials.*

Have you been yearning for some cherished goal to come to fruition? Are you beginning to despair and lose hope that it will ever come true?

Ask yourself:

"Have I prayed about my goal— mentally pictured it as already accomplished, and given it to God to bring about in the right way according to that Higher Will?"

If you have, then remind yourself that:

God's delays are not God's denials.

You may be in a holding pattern waiting for all things to come together in perfect timing. Or the delay may be a blessing in disguise, and a greater good is being prepared for you. It may also be that your goal is ego-driven and God is trying to redirect you to something better.

In any case, be patient in your faith and give the goal back to God. Replace your anxiety and negative mental scenarios with the serenity of total trust in God. Surrender your desire with the prayer:

> *Trusting and resting,*
> *I place my desire in your loving hands.*
> *Let it be this or something better, Lord,*
> *according to you Will for my highest good.*
> *Let Thy will be done.*

TODAY, I AM GRATEFUL FOR: _____

_____

GOD'S DAY 93 — *Healing*

Remember, _____,
(speak your name aloud)

—that the radiant Life of God is at the center
of every atom and cell of your body temple.

When you are feeling ill, call your mind up higher and picture your body aglow with the radiant life and health of God.

Take your mind off the appearances and concentrate on the healing idea that:

Mighty currents of God's healing love
are flowing through me now,
healing and restoring me,
and I am grateful!
Thank You, God!

Bless your body and speak lovingly to it as you would a child—for it is the child of your creation, and depends upon you for its love and support.

Today, remember to bless your body temple with love!

*TODAY, I AM GRATEFUL FOR:*_____

_____

GOD'S DAY 94 — *Success*

Remember, _____,
                    (speak your name aloud)

> *—you are programmed for success.*

Your Creator has placed a perfect operating system at the core of your being. You are programmed for life, love, joy, and success.

Through ignorance and fear you have overridden this original program and entered self-defeating data. Society has also slipped "viruses" of failure and confusion into your operating system.

In your quiet time of prayer now, ask your Wise and Loving Creator to erase this wrong programming and bring forth the confident Self that is your true nature.

Charles Fillmore's "Invocation" is a beautiful prayer to use for this purpose.

> *"I am now in the presence of pure Being,*
> *and immersed in the Holy Spirit of life,*
> *love, and wisdom.*
> *I acknowledge Thy presence and Thy power,*
> *O Blessed Spirit;*
> *in Thy divine wisdom*
> *now erase my mortal limitations*
> *and from Thy pure substance of love*
> *bring into manifestation my world,*
> *according to Thy perfect law."* [4]

TODAY, I AM GRATEFUL FOR: _____

_____

GOD'S DAY 95 — *Supply*

Remember, _____,
          (speak your name aloud)

—God always has, always will, and is now
providing for you on every level of your being.

It is easy to start imagining the worst-case scenarios of lack and limitation. Soon your mind is sliding downhill into despair.

When you feel yourself falling into that negativity, quickly counteract those thoughts with this powerful statement:

God always has, always will,
and is now providing for me
on every level of my being
and I am grateful!
I have plenty to use, plenty to share,
and plenty to spare!
Thank You, God!

Hold firm to this truth, and new avenues of prosperity will open to you!

*TODAY, I AM GRATEFUL FOR:*_____

_____

GOD'S DAY 96 — *Let God Take Charge*

Remember, _____,
             (speak your name aloud)

        —to let God take charge of your day.

    As you awaken and swing your legs out of bed, start your day with these words:

Spirit, make my day!

Make it as You desire it to be for my highest good.

Make my day Yours, not mine.

As you begin your work, pray:

Spirit, make my day!

Take the lead and I will follow.

Let me be your instrument.

Let this day accomplish Your purposes through me.

I let Spirit make my day, and I know it's going to be good!

TODAY, I AM GRATEFUL FOR: _____

_____

Let Me Be a Blessing

Beloved Lord,
You created me for Your own.
I am Yours.

Your love makes me infinitely worthy,
and in Your eyes I am unique and priceless.

It is my joy to serve You
and be a blessing to Your world today.

I open my heart to You. Show me how to serve You—
how to be an instrument for You to work through,
love through, and create through.

I place myself in the synchronicity
of Your grace today.

Set my day in order,
that all may be in perfect sequence
to accomplish Your purposes, not mine.

Let me be a blessing instrument for You today.

GOD'S DAY 97 — *Inside Job*

Remember, _____,
(speak your name aloud)

—your work is not something you do.
It is something done through you. It is an inside job.

Your right way of working is to be in partnership with the Creative Intelligence within you.

Today, take that Creative Intelligence as your Senior Life Partner. Let It supply the ideas, as you do the leg work.

Your main task in this inner Partnership is to listen to that voice of intuition speaking softly in the background behind the chatter of your worldly ego thoughts. Then simply follow through as directed.

Periodically during the day, ask this question:

Who's doing this work?

This will remind you that it is not you, but your Inner Partner that is directing and doing the work through you. Your daily duties will flow along in perfect sequence and perfect order.

As Jesus said,

"… the Father that dwells in me, he does the work."
—John 14:10

TODAY, I AM GRATEFUL FOR: _____

_____

GOD'S DAY 98 — Heaven or Hell

Remember, _____,
      (speak your name aloud)

—you make your own heaven and you make your own hell.
You get to choose which it will be.

You make your own heaven here on Earth with every thought, attitude, and action, and you make your own hell the same way.

Heaven and hell are states of consciousness, although you may call them places if you prefer. Because after you leave your Earthly house, your body—you go on to live in a "house not made with hands"—a house of consciousness.

Every time you choose love instead of fear you are building a heavenly house to live in here as well as in the spiritual life beyond. Every time you choose forgiveness instead of judgment and hatred, you are building heaven for yourself.

There are infinite levels of consciousness—from the deepest hell to the highest most celestial heaven. But no matter which level is yours, God is there, shining Light and Love upon you to light your way.

Whither shall I go from thy Spirit?
Or whither shall I flee from thy presence?
If I ascend up into heaven, thou art there;
if I make my bed in hell behold thou art there.
Psalm 139:7, 8

Today choose your thoughts wisely for you are creating your own heaven, your own hell.

TODAY, I AM GRATEFUL FOR: _____

GOD'S DAY 99 — *Grieving*

Remember, _____,

(speak your name aloud)

*—in the midst of grief there are two truths
that will lift you out of sorrow.*

They were given to a man by his beloved wife in her final days before passing. Whenever he felt the tears welling up in his eyes, he would remember these two statements.

"I bring forward all of the best, and I let go of the rest."

"I am so grateful!"

These two ideas kept him afloat. He brought forward all of the best memories and let go of the unhappy ones.

Instead he focused on being grateful for all the good years they had enjoyed together.

Every day he reminded himself to be grateful for everything and everyone in his life for that day.

In the midst of your own grief—whether it is the loss of a loved one, a divorce, or any other life experience that is causing you to grieve, remember to—

*Bring forward all of the best and let go of the rest,
and remember to be grateful!*

TODAY, I AM GRATEFUL FOR: _____
_____

GOD'S DAY 100 — *Seeking Your Good*

Remember, _____,

> (speak your name aloud)

> *—the good you are seeking is seeking you!*

It is so easy to fall into the trap of thinking that you must search hard for the good that Life has for you—as if it were being kept from you.

You know there is good for you and you are going to have it! So you wrinkle your brow, you grit your teeth, and go in hot pursuit of what you think is "your good."

The truth is, if you will simply slow down, relax, and lift your vision to the Source of all Good, you would find that the Good you seek is seeking you!

Good is a Name for God, and God is ever with you, ever aware of your needs and desires.

> *Before they call, I will answer, says the Lord. . .and while they are yet speaking, I will hear.* Isaiah 65:24

Today remember that the Good you are pursuing so intently is also seeking you!

Hold this thought for yourself today:

> *The Good that I am seeking is seeking me!*
> *I claim it now and give thanks for it!*

*TODAY, I AM GRATEFUL FOR:*_____

_____

GOD'S DAY 101 — *Agree with Change*

Remember, _____,

        (speak your name aloud)

          —life is change.

Jesus said:

Agree with your adversary while you are in the way with him, lest he deliver you to the judge and the judge deliver you to prison...

The "adversary" that we are resisting may well be a change that our personal self perceives as frightening or unwelcome.

Cease resenting and resisting, and instead ask God to show you the good hidden in the change.

Let go and let the change move you on to the new good that God has for you.

Do this now in your quiet time.

Loving Lord, help me to let go of my unwillingness and fear.
Let this change move me forward to the new good
that You are bringing forth from this change.
Show me the blessing in it.

TODAY, I AM GRATEFUL FOR: _____

_____

GOD'S DAY 102 — *Creativity*

Remember, _____,
 (speak your name aloud)

*—deep within you is a pure, clear spring of creativity
and inspiration.*

Like a hidden spring in a forest lying beneath layers of leaves, so your creativity may be covered over with mental and emotional debris.

But if you are willing to kneel down and clear away all of the leaves—your old fears, and counter-productive attitudes— the springs of your creative potential will gush forth with new energy and success.

"Kneeling down" means being willing to surrender your self-centered will and your self-limiting beliefs.

Four major inner blocks clog the springs of your success and creativity: lack of self-worth; old resentments; attachment to limiting work roles and identities; and four, fear of change and its possible consequences.

Examine each one and see which one is the most relevant in your life right now.

Today close your eyes and visualize kneeling down by the inner springs of your creativity and clearing away the debris. Let your prayer be:

*Indwelling Lord, help me to release these negative attitudes,
and clear the way for my creativity to spring forth
and express itself.*

TODAY, I AM GRATEFUL FOR: _____

GOD'S DAY 103 — Self-Renewal

Remember, _____,
(speak your name aloud)

—to go to the beach before sunrise when all the Earth is quiet—
if only in your imagination today.

Be alone with the great ocean, the Mother of all life. Watch as the Earth awakens and turns to greet the sun to receive its blessing.

Greet the Sun with a prayer of gratitude, and begin your barefoot walk in the edge of the surf.

On days when you are feeling pressured and troubled with stress, give it all to the ocean and let the out-flowing waves carry it out to sea.

In your meditation today, imagine dropping your fears and pressures into the ocean of God's Love.

Let them be washed away.

Feel free and restored.

*TODAY, I AM GRATEFUL FOR:*_____

_____

GOD'S DAY 104 — Thank You

Remember, _____,

        (speak your name aloud)

    —to make today a *Moment-of-Thanks* day!

Ask yourself:

Who and what in my life are am I taking for granted?

Take a moment to thank your body temple that struggles to serve you well, despite your neglect of it.

Take a moment to thank your spouse, or your parents, or friends that support you and encourage you.

And do not overlook the beautiful sunrise that you often miss admiring, or the bird that soars, silhouetted against the brilliant flame of the sunset.

It only takes a minute to speak a heart-felt thank you.

Make today a *Moment-of-Thanks* day!

TODAY, I AM GRATEFUL FOR: _____

_____

GOD'S DAY 105 — *God's Plan*

Remember, _____,
          (speak your name aloud)

God has a plan for your life.

You do not have to know everything in advance.
You only need to keep moving ahead
one step at a time,
knowing that the way is being made clear.

God has a plan for your life.

Know that your Higher Power
is working through you to accomplish whatever
is for your highest good.
Relax in this knowing.

God has a plan for your life.

Keep your eyes open for opportunities to serve.
Keep your ears open for guidance.
Stop fretting and start letting
God be in charge.

Listen, obey, and enjoy!

*TODAY, I AM GRATEFUL FOR:*_____

_____

GOD'S DAY 106 — *Guidance*

Remember, _____,
(speak your name aloud)

—to ask yourself: *Who is running my life?*

And conversely, *Am I trying to run someone else's life?*

Trying to run someone else's life won't work because you neither have the right nor wisdom to do so.

They have their own life's path to walk, and it is uniquely theirs because as they walk that path they will meet the experiences and lessons they need for their soul's growth.

The only "someone else" you want to run your life is your Higher Power—the wisdom and power of God within you.

Your personal ego, driven by its fears and desires, has not the wisdom to safely navigate the hero's journey that you have embarked upon in this life.

Like the knights of old, who were always guided by a wisdom figure on their quest, your Inner Christ will guide you safely on your journey.

Today, take time to listen to that Higher Wisdom.

TODAY, I AM GRATEFUL FOR: _____

_____

GOD'S DAY 107 — Happiness

Remember, _____,

       (speak your name aloud)

      —happiness is an inside job.

Have you taken responsibility for your life, or are you continually looking outside yourself for situations or people to blame for what you are experiencing?

The moment you realize *"I am responsible for my life"* —in that very moment you will take charge and make the changes in your thinking that will change your life for the better! *Happiness is an inside job.*

Today, examine the attitudes and beliefs you are holding. Weed out all the negative ones, for they only bring a harvest of unhappiness.

Begin now cultivating positive attitudes —for *misery is self-inflicted, and happiness is self-bestowed!*

Today, look at yourself with eyes of love and total worthiness. Be grateful for God's Good in your life.

Remember, you make your own world, and happiness is found within.

TODAY, I AM GRATEFUL FOR: _____

GOD'S DAY 108 — *Soul's Journey*

Remember, _____,

      (speak your name aloud)

—your soul's story is worthy of a bestseller. Mine it.

No one else has quite the same life as yours with its unique journey through childhood experiences, wounds and revelations, laughter and tears.

Your soul chose this journey before you came into this world—this classroom, this proving ground for soul mastery.

Your life is a soul portrait still in progress. Step back from your work and gain perspective by writing down your story.

It is a masterpiece, and others are waiting to read it to gain courage for their own journey.

Begin writing your life story today.

Write in the third person as if you were writing a novel, and greater insights will come forth as you spin out the story.

TODAY, I AM GRATEFUL FOR: _____

GOD'S DAY 109 — Attitudes

Remember, _____,
         (speak your name aloud)

   —attitudes are contagious. Are yours worth catching?

   —or should you be quarantined for that terrible infectious gloom you are spreading?

   The fastest way to cure a bad case of emotional infection is to begin reciting *I am grateful* over and over like a mantra.

   No state of gloom, no case of self-pity can survive a concentrated attack of gratitude mantras.

   The mind is forced to shift out of its gloom, and once that shift has occurred, your heart will fill with peace, light, and joy.

   Today, practice your *I am grateful* mantra.

*TODAY, I AM GRATEFUL FOR:*_____

_____

GOD'S DAY 110 — *Intention*

Remember, _____,

      (speak your name aloud)

> *—this brand new day is waiting for you*
> *to declare your intent.*

What kind of a day do you want it to become?

Is it going to be: *"…one of those days,"*

Or is it going to be:

> *"I can hardly wait to see the good God*
> *has in store for me today!"*

The universe is always listening. It will deliver according to your declaration of intention today.

Today, I set my intention to _____.

I declare today to be a _____day!

GOD'S DAY 111 — Stay Connected

Remember, _____,

> (speak your name aloud)

> *—to stay connected to Source today.*

Have you ever vacuumed the carpet and pulled the cord too tightly as you tried to reach beyond the cord's length? The plug yanked out of the electrical outlet, and the motor shut off! The connection was broken.

Life is like that. Stress and tension break our mental connection with God, our Power Source.

When you are feeling "strung out" take time to remember your oneness with the Power Source.

Right now, relax and reconnect in your mind with the Source of Peace, Love, and Power.

> *Loving Lord, take my hand that I may be reconnected*
> *to Your Love, Your Peace, and Your Power*

*TODAY, I AM GRATEFUL FOR:*_____

GOD'S DAY 112 — *Trusting in God*

Remember, _____,

(speak your name aloud)

—when you are struggling with self-doubt, think of these words:

I trust the process of life.

All I need is always taken care of.

I am safe.

These words were found hand-printed in white paint on the sidewalk, approaching a bridge in Florida.

Who had written this mysterious message? Why had they written it at the bridge? Were they contemplating suicide, and had shored up their faith with these words?

We will never know, but whenever you are feeling overwhelmed, remind yourself of that powerful message.

You are never alone. The Presence is always with you. Truly you can trust in the process of life, and rely on your Higher Power to take care of you and keep you safe.

Remind yourself:

I trust the process of life.
All I need is always taken care of.
I am safe.

TODAY, I AM GRATEFUL FOR: _____

_____

GOD'S DAY 113 — *Your Yes Power*

Remember, _____,
　　　　　(speak your name aloud)
—to use your "Yes" power wisely.

What are you saying 'Yes" to in your life? Look around your home, your work environment, and at the people in your life. Look around inside your house of consciousness.

Whatever you have in your life is the result of your saying "Yes" to it—either consciously or subconsciously, or by default by not rejecting it.

Are you saying *"Yes"* to abundance or to lack? Order or disorder? Self-doubt or self-confidence?

Consciously say *"No"* to anything undesirable in your life, and "Yes" to the things, people, and conditions that you would really love to bring into your life.

The universe is always saying, *"Yes"* to you—meaning that whatever you imagine, accept, and desire, the universe will work to bring into your life by the great Law of Mind Action.

Today, speak these words to yourself:

I say No to lack, and limitation
I say No to feelings of unworthiness or doubt.
I say Yes to abundance and good health,
I say Yes to loving relationships, and success.

*TODAY, I AM GRATEFUL FOR:*_____

_____

GOD'S DAY 114 — *Light Source*

Remember, _____,

(speak your name aloud)

Each of us is like a stained glass window in a beautiful cathedral.

The Light Source is the same for all of us, but our particular soul makeup has its own unique characteristic and color. We are each beautiful in our own right—not one more beautiful than the next.

Unfortunately, our negative emotions show up in colors too—dark, murky gray, angry red.

Today, in your meditation, make the stained glass window of your soul shine with bright joy, peaceful blue, and the clear gold of creativity!

Go into the sacred chapel of your soul and gaze upon the stained glass window with God's Light and Love shining through.

TODAY, I AM GRATEFUL FOR: _____

GOD'S DAY 115 — *New Openings*

Remember, _____,

      (speak your name aloud)

—to break out of the rut of mindless habitual living.

Today deliberately chose do things differently.

Eat a different breakfast, change your dressing routine, take a different route to work.

Change your work routine.

Let there be cracks in your old patterns that open the way for new opportunities to squeeze through—new openings for the fabled princes of serendipity to gift you with unexpected blessings.

Take a moment now to ask your Higher Self:

What new doors are you opening for me today?
What new ways of working do you want me to try today?

*TODAY, I AM GRATEFUL FOR:*_____

GOD'S DAY 116 — *The School of Life*

Remember, _____,
                            (speak your name aloud)

> *—everyone gets out of this life alive!*

Think not that when your body dies, you die too.

That would be the waste of a perfectly good soul, and God is too good an Environmentalist to allow that—and too good a Headmaster not to make sure that you finish your education.

In this change called death, your soul simply takes a vacation break from this boarding school called life. Your course of study for this term will be over. Your soul returns to its heavenly home to rest, relax, and think things over.

It sees what courses it did well in, and which you need to take over. The Headmaster will help you lay out a new course of study in the basic "three Rs" of life:

Relationships—making them work with love.

Responsibility—for your thoughts and actions.

Reverence—for God, and the Spirit of God in
  all persons, and the oneness of all life.

Next term you will enroll in a higher grade, working with these same "three Rs" but on a higher level of understanding.

In the meantime, enjoy your schooldays here, and apply yourself to your lessons.

TODAY, I AM GRATEFUL FOR: _____

_____

GOD'S DAY 117 — *Divine Order*

Remember, _____,
(speak your name aloud)

—to declare *Divine Order* for yourself and your activities today:

Let there be Divine Order today!
Let there be a perfect outworking in all of my activities today.

Order is the first law of the universe, and when you invoke *Divine Order* you are putting yourself and your affairs into synchronization with the perfect flow of that great Law.

Speak *Divine Order* when you are making airline connections, or when your business projects are not working out right, or when you have lost something in the house. Miraculously, in a few moments you will be led to where that object is.

Claim *Divine Order* for healing discords in your body temple.

Claim *Divine Order* to heal inharmonies in your personal relationships.

Put *Divine Order* to work for you today.

Let your prayer be:

Let there be Divine Order today!
Let there be a perfect outworking
in all of my activities today."

*TODAY, I AM GRATEFUL FOR:*_____

_____

GOD'S DAY 118 — *Healing Wounds*

Remember, _____,
(speak your name aloud)

—it doesn't help to scratch the wound.
It only makes it worse.

And that goes for emotional wounds as well.

Have you noticed that the more you finger the hurt in your mind, the worse it disturbs your peace?

Some people like to rehearse the hurt over and over. They appear to get some kind of miserable pleasure from telling the story repeatedly. But they never seem to get better. They never heal and move on with their life.

Dress the wound with a salve of love and acceptance, and bandage it with forgiveness of yourself and the other person involved.

Then let it be.

Bless it and forget about it. It will heal on its own.

Today, if you have such an old wound—dress it and forget it.

Get on with life
and the good that God has waiting for you.

TODAY, I AM GRATEFUL FOR: _____

_____

GOD'S DAY 119 — *Son-Light*

Remember, _____,
(speak your name aloud)

—you are only here to let the Son shine through.
Beyond the ego's fear of abandonment,
beyond its self-hatred and self-condemnation,
is the beautiful and radiant Self.

Beyond the ego's pride and inability
to admit it is wrong,
beyond its anger and its rage,
beyond its whimperings and whining,
and feelings of inadequacy—
is that great and love-filled Self,
ever radiating Love, Light and Joy,
shining its Light upon the earth of your life.

You here only to let the Son shine through your soul.
Keep its surfaces clean
of fear and doubt
Clear away the soot of pride,
stubbornness, and willfulness,
so that the Light within you can shine forth
to light the way for those who walk in darkness.

Today, remember to let your Son Light shine!

*TODAY, I AM GRATEFUL FOR:*_____

_____

GOD'S DAY 120 — Abundance

Remember, _____,
        (speak your name aloud)

> *—all that you need for your daily living comes*
> *in a continuous supply from the Father's hand.*

In your meditation today, look at your hands and see a golden stream of shining substance pouring through them from on High.

Cup your hands and gratefully receive this overflowing supply of Inexhaustible Goodness. Feel it in your palms.

Now see that Supply forming into the specific desire. Take hold of it, and give thanks for it. It is yours.

Let this be your prayer;

> *All that the Father has is mine to use and to share,*
> *and I am grateful.*

TODAY, I AM GRATEFUL FOR: _____

_____

GOD'S DAY 121 — Partnership with God

Remember, _____,
(speak your name aloud)

—to kick out the "I."

Enough of: "I'm going to do this, I'm going to do that."
I . . . I . . . I . . . me . . . me . . . me . . .

Forget yourself today.

Leave your "I" and "me" behind.

Go through today as *"we."*

God and I, God and me.

Do everything with God today.

Think *"we."*

Ask:

What are we going to do together today, Lord?

What do you have planned for us today, Beloved?

What fun? What joy?

Kick out the 'I' today and join hands with your Beloved!

*TODAY, I AM GRATEFUL FOR:*_____

_____

GOD'S DAY 122 — *Gratitude*

Remember, _____,
(speak your name aloud)

—to practice saying "Thank You, God!"
throughout the day for everything that happens,
regardless of whether or not it appears to be good.

Your praise acts like a magnet to draw forth God's Good even in 'thankless' situations, because the goodness of God is everywhere present waiting to be recognized.

Your gratitude has the power to shift energy from negative to positive. It changes the chemical balance in your body from toxic to healthy. Discouragement and depression cannot survive a powerful dose of genuine gratitude.

When you are having difficulty with someone, try silently repeating:

"I praise the goodness of God in you."

In a few minutes you will find your negative feelings dissolving as praise "lightens up" the entire situation and gives you peace.

Today, practice gratitude!

TODAY, I AM GRATEFUL FOR: _____

_____

GOD'S DAY 123 — *Refiner's Fire*

Remember, _____,
(speak your name aloud)

—*in the Secret Place of the Most High in your spiritual heart burns the Holy Fire of God's Infinite Love.*

Nothing can exist in that All-consuming Flame but the Holy Flame Itself.

No disease, no fear, no hatred, nor inharmony can survive there.

In your meditation now commit all that concerns you to that purifying Flame. Let the Refiner's Fire burn up the dross of your life.

Commit yourself to that sacred Flame until you become one with that All-consuming Love.

Today, I commit myself, my life, and all that concerns me to the Fire of God's Infinite Love.

*TODAY, I AM GRATEFUL FOR:*_____

GOD'S DAY 124 — Light-Bringer

Remember, _____,
(speak your name aloud)

—you are a Light-Bringer.

The world needs your Light to find its way out of the darkness of fear, violence, and materialism.

When you hear of something in the news that is disturbing, mentally send Christ Light and Love to the persons involved.

Jesus gives us the right response—"Be not overcome with evil, but overcome evil (or darkness) with good."

As you send forth strong thoughts of Divine Love, you can dissipate the darkness!

In your quiet time now, visualize sending forth that Light and Love. Imagine it spreading forth through your home, through the neighborhood, blessing all in its path.

Send it farther to our nation's leaders, continuing on around the world to the places of strife, spreading peace and comfort in its path.

Let your Light shine.
You are the light of the world.

TODAY, I AM GRATEFUL FOR: _____

_____

GOD'S DAY 125 — *Life's Purpose*

Remember, _____,
　　　　　　(speak your name aloud)

> *"He who finds his life shall lose it,*
> *and he who loses his life for my sake shall find it."*
> Matthew 10:39

　It sounds like a paradox, an impossibility, and yet it is the truth!

　Jesus was saying that he that is concerned only for saving his own skin shall lose it. Only as you lose yourself in a cause or purpose greater that yourself can you find the complete fulfillment you desire.

　Ask yourself:

> *In what am I investing my life?*
> *Is it of lasting value?*
> *Will it make a difference in the world?*

Open yourself to the leadings of your Higher Self who is waiting to lead you into your life's purpose.

Let your prayer be:

> *Loving Lord, help me to invest my life in ways*
> *that will fulfill the purposes you have for me.*

TODAY, I AM GRATEFUL FOR: _____

_____

GOD'S DAY 126 — *Prosperity*

Remember, _____,
> (speak your name aloud)

> *—true prosperity is not a rich bank account.*
> *It is the rich consciousness behind the bank account.*

If you are facing a financial problem, remember where your true security comes from.

It does not come from outer things—jobs, stock market and the like—for these may fail. Trust instead in the All-providing Presence of God. New channels of supply will open unto you.

Your consciousness is like a magnet that will draw your good to you, or conversely, lack, if you have a lack consciousness.

In your quiet time now, hold the following truths to begin building a new consciousness of God as your infinite and unfailing supply:

> *I have faith in God as my instant,*
> *constant and abundant supply.*
> *I have faith in God to open ways where*
> *to human sense there appears no way.*

> *I follow God's promptings and new avenues*
> *of prosperity are opening to me now.*
> *Thank You. Spirit!*

TODAY, I AM GRATEFUL FOR: _____

_____

GOD'S DAY 127 — *False Labels*

Remember, _____,
> (speak your name aloud)

> *—to put a new label on yourself today!*

We live our lives under the stigmas of the labels that we, and society, have placed upon us.

These judgments describe us on every level of our life— our physical appearance, our career, failures and successes, skin color, culture, marital status, and a hundred other labels.

When we accept these judgments as true about ourselves, we stifle our creativity and limit our potential to be all that we were created to be.

Remember, you are much more than you appear to be. You are endowed by your Creator with wondrous gifts and potentials that you haven't yet tapped.

Hold this truth for yourself:

> *I am more than I appear to be.*
> *I am a strong, capable, and wise individual,*
> *bringing forth the best that God has placed in me.*

TODAY, I AM GRATEFUL FOR: _____

GOD'S DAY 128 — *New Start*

Remember, _____,
              (speak your name aloud)

         —today could be your last day.

Don't misunderstand. While it could be your last day on Earth— (and if it is, what are you doing with it in terms of expressing God's love?)

—but it could also be your last day to be stuck in the rut of your self-pity and negativity.

It could be your last day addicted to a self-destructive habit.

It could be your last day of lack and delay.

It could be your last day stuck in a self-limiting career or relationship.

It could be the last day before you break out into the light, joy and freedom of a new life!

Make today the *last* day of your old life!

Make today the *first* day of the new you!

In your meditation focus on this thought:

Today I start a new life working with God as my Partner.
Today I start a new life in Christ!

TODAY, I AM GRATEFUL FOR: _____

_____

GOD'S DAY 129 — *Wake Up Call*

Remember, _____,
       (speak your name aloud)

—the 2 x 4 between the eyes will come
as many times as you need it.

Every accident, every illness, every crisis—is a 2 x 4 wake up call, calling us back to our true path and purpose.

Sometimes we need that 2 x 4 several times until we finally get the message. It may come in different ways, health challenges, career failures, relationship difficulties, but they are all trying to awaken us to the same message.

If we do not express what we came to express, create what we came to create, and share the love that we are—then that creativity and love, in its struggle to be born, will create internal havoc in our mind and body, and external havoc in our affairs.

Stop and take a long hard look at the crises in your life. Look beyond the outer disguise to the inner meaning.

You will find something is way out of balance. Some deep and important part of you in being squelched or ignored. Your mind and your heart are not tracking together. Somewhere a connection has been broken with your Power Source.

Today, in your mediation ask God some important questions:

What is this 2 x 4, this crisis, trying to tell me? Where is
my life out of balance? Where am I not loving myself and
honoring my true direction and talents? Why am I not express-
ing my deepest desires to express and create?

*TODAY, I AM GRATEFUL FOR:*_____

GOD'S DAY 130 — *Take Time*

Remember, _____,
(speak your name aloud)

—to rest in your heart today.

In the midst of your daily pressures and duties, take a moment to put your hand on your heart and rest there.

Just for a moment let your hurried thoughts return to the Secret Place of the Most High in your spiritual heart.

Just for a moment silently say:

Right here, right now, God is . . . and all is well.

That is all it takes to reconnect with God's Peace and Power for your day.

Today, in your busy activities take time to remember:

Right here, right now, God is . . . and all is well.

TODAY, I AM GRATEFUL FOR: _____
_____

GOD'S DAY 131 — *Recovery*

Remember, _____,
           (speak your name aloud)

—all true and lasting recovery is spiritual.

If you trying to recover from an addiction, know you can't make it on your own. You don't know how and even if you did, your habitual mind is too filled with self-defeating thoughts and attitudes to be of any help.

Most people who use alcohol or drugs are very spiritual people who intuitively sense that there is a Power that can give them the peace, love and joy they desperately seek. But not being in touch with their spiritual nature where this Power resides, they seek escape in the power of chemicals to give them counterfeit peace.

When you say, "I am a recovering (alcoholic/drug addict/overeater/etc.)"—you are usually speaking in the context of recovering *from* your addiction. But ask yourself: What is it that I am trying *to* recover?

What you are really trying to recover is the peace of mind that can only come from letting that loving Higher Power take charge of your life and restore you to happiness and well being.

This Power is the pearl hidden in the oyster of your dysfunctional ego. It took the hard knock of hitting bottom in your addiction to crack open your ego's hard shell. Let go, and let that Something Greater take over now. Remind yourself:

God is my habit, I need no other.

TODAY, I AM GRATEFUL FOR:_____

Prayer Letter To an Alcoholic

The Truth about you is that you are more than an alcoholic,
you are more than a failure, you are more than a victim.
You are more than a powerless person.
You do not have to drink because you feel powerless.
The real Truth about you is that you are eternal—
a power-filled, beloved child of the Infinite.
You are useful, worthy and creative.
Looking with eyes of God's Love,
I see you and behold you that way now.

Deep down beneath all of the difficulties and growing pains, lies
your eternal soul on its path of spiritual evolution and awakening.

Your soul is like the seed of a beautiful flower buried beneath
a rubbish heap. When the sunlight seeps through and awakens the
life in the seed, it begins to grow and push up through the debris into
the full brilliance of the sunlight—free, beautiful and stately, unsoiled
by anything around it.

Every adverse condition in life—once overcome, serves as a
nourishing reminder of your spiritual victory. It becomes that which
helped you to grow and awaken to your true nature.

Awake or asleep, intoxicated or sober, the Son-light of your Higher
Power's Love is shining upon you. At the right time you will feel that
warmth and respond. You will awaken to the realization of your
rightful purpose in life.

You will sense the power and potential your Creator has endowed
you with and placed deep within you. You will emerge out of the old
husk, shake off your old fears and doubts, and grow into the
beautiful person your Creator created you to be.

Let your Higher Power unwrap the grave clothes of old fears.
hurts, self-pity and guilt, and free you with His Love.
I now release you into His care and keeping.
I love you and bless you, and call forth the Best in you.
You begin a new cycle of freedom and spiritual growth now!

GOD'S DAY 132 — Something Greater

Remember, _____,
               (speak your name aloud)

    —when you are feeling overwhelmed or troubled, know that:

*There is Something Greater in you
that has the Wisdom, the Power, and the Love
to lift you out of your difficulties.*

*There is Something Greater
that knows the Way,
and will lead you safely through to peace and joy.*

*That Something Greater
is the vital and loving Presence of God within you
ever shining, ever waiting to love you and lift you,
and give you Peace.*

*To reach It you need only to take a deep breath,
and whisper silently to yourself;
"I am Part of Something Greater.
I am a beloved child of God.
I am safe, I am free. All is well.*

TODAY, I AM GRATEFUL FOR: _____

_____

GOD'S DAY 133 — *Power to Change*

Remember, _____,
                (speak your name aloud)

—you have the power to choose your thoughts,
and the power to choose your thoughts is the power
to change your life.

Remember, every mental image—every thought held in mind—is the engine of change; it is the seed of a new harvest of consequences.

What consequences do you want to set into motion today? What are you choosing for yourself today? Set your intention with the following statements:

Today, I choose to be_____

Today, I choose to have_____

Today, I choose to feel_____

Today, I choose to think_____

Today, I choose to love_____

Today, I choose to act_____

TODAY, I AM GRATEFUL FOR: _____
_____

GOD'S DAY 134 — *Serenity*

Remember, _____,
(speak your name aloud)

*—the secret of serenity
is to keep your mind on your Higher Power.*

Your habitual mind is like an untrained dog that loves to dig up garbage from the past, or gnaw on future worry bones.

Speak *"Stay"* to it.

Call it back to the present moment by saying,

"Right here, right now."

Let it rest in the peace of God.

Form the habit of carrying on an inner conversation with that loving Power during your daily activities.

Invite It to be your moment-by-moment guide. Healing or recovery is accomplished one moment at a time, by keeping your mind on your Higher Power. The present moment is the moment of power.

The more your mind is focused on your Higher Power, the less your thoughts drift off into trouble. Soon your new mental habit will automatically keep your mind focused on God's ever-present help, love, and peace.

Let your prayer be:

*Right here, right now,
I am centered in God's Peace.*

*TODAY, I AM GRATEFUL FOR:*_____
_____

GOD'S DAY 135 — *Breath of the Almighty*

Remember, _____,
(speak your name aloud)

"The spirit of God has made me, and the breath of the
Almighty has given me life."
Job 33:4

In your quiet time today, meditate on that *"breath of the Almighty."*

Take a deep slow breath as you speak these words:

Beloved Lord, I breathe Thee in,
Beloved Lord, I breathe Thee out,
and in between I rest in Thy Presence.

Hear God's Voice answering;

Beloved Child, I breathe thee in,
Beloved Child, I breathe thee out,
and in between you rest in my Heart.

Repeat, and a third time. Feel God's Presence.

Rest in God's heart.

TODAY, I AM GRATEFUL FOR: _____
_____

GOD'S DAY 136 — *Oneness*

Remember, _____,
(speak your name aloud)

> *—you are not one, but many,*
> *and you are many becoming one.*

You have many selves—many sub-personalities that make up the whole of you. Each is vying for your attention.

They all play their roles on your life's stage.

There is the child and the parent, the lover and the rejected, the winner and the loser, the brave and the timid, the worker and the loafer, the nurturer and the taker, the aggressor and the peacemaker, the pray-er and the scoffer, the materialist and the spiritual master.

Today, in your meditation, bring them all under the direction of the Master Director—your Higher Self.

Imagine a spotlight of God's Light and Love.

Call into the Light each of these many aspects of yourself.

Consecrate each to the service of the Christ within. Let them receive the blessing and the direction of that Master Self.

Let the many be integrated into the One.

*TODAY, I AM GRATEFUL FOR:*_____

GOD'S DAY 137 — *Fill the Chalice*

Remember, _____,

(speak your name aloud)

—to take care of yourself.
You are the chalice from which others drink.

You are the chalice from which others refresh their spirits and revive themselves. Take care not to be drawn down and depleted. Your light, love and strength comes from the great fountain of God's strength within you.

In your meditation now, see yourself walking down a beautiful forest path. Tall trees arch overhead forming a green canopy. Ahead you see a clearing, with a small white chapel shining in the sun.

Step inside the cool dark interior. Down front the altar is illuminated by a shaft of sunlight coming through a skylight. Upon the altar, catching the sun's rays, is a golden chalice filled with God's Love and Peace.

In reverence now, drink from that chalice.

Fill your heart and refresh your soul.

Let your prayer be:

Loving Lord, fill me with your Spirit.
Fill me with your Wisdom, your Peace, and your Strength
until my cup runs over and I share with all those in need today.

TODAY, I AM GRATEFUL FOR: _____

_____

GOD'S DAY 138 — *Free Yourself*

Remember, _____,
            (speak your name aloud)

—you don't have to suffer another minute
of gloom, guilt, fear or hurt.
The Christ within you has the power to set you free.

In your meditation now, relax your muscles, and watch your body breathe for a few moments.

Now, imagine being in the presence of the Christ. Reach into your heart and pull out all of the negative emotions, fear, anger, loneliness, guilt that hide in the dark corners. Imagine rolling them up into a dark gray ball. Hand the ball to the radiant Christ and ask that it be transformed.

Visualize the Christ transforming the ball into a glowing, radiant golden ball of peace and love, and handing it back you. Clasp the golden ball of peace and love to your heart and breathe it into your heart.

Breathe that light and love quietly for a few moments. Relax in peace and gratitude.

Then call yourself back to the present and slowly open your eyes. You will find the negative energy has been transmuted and you are free.

TODAY, I AM GRATEFUL FOR: _____

_____

GOD'S DAY 139 — *Imagination*

Remember, _____,
(speak your name aloud)

—arm-wrestling between your willpower and your imagination always results in a broken willpower.

Your imagination will always overpower your willpower. If you imagine yourself indulging a harmful habit, you will soon be hooked by it, even if you try to resist it.

Instead of wrestling with it, simply imagine yourself doing an alternative positive activity. Your imagination will go to work to steer you to that healthy alternative. Keep handy in your mind a favorite alternative image that you can immediately substitute for the addictive image.

It may be the thought of someone you love. A young father, when he was tempted to indulge a harmful habit, substituted the image of his young son, whom he loved dearly and for whom he wanted to be worthy father. As he kept his thoughts on his son, he was able to steer himself away from temptation.

You may want to picture a favorite place in nature that brings a sense of peace to you. Put your mind on that place. See yourself there.

Try it now in your quiet time. Select the image you have chosen, and practice being there. Feel the emotion of it. The more strongly you fix that image in your heart, the more it will serve you in times of temptation.

TODAY, I AM GRATEFUL FOR: _____

_____

GOD'S DAY 140 — *Let God Be in Charge*

Remember, _____,

        (speak your name aloud)

           —to let God be God in your life.

What would happen aboard ship if the crewmen did not let the captain be the captain...or in an orchestra if the musicians did not let the conductor be the conductor?

What would happen on the football field if the players did not let the coach be the coach?

There would be chaos, and lack of direction.

So, too, when you declare God to be in charge, let it be so. Let God be your captain, your conductor, and coach.

Let go of your fears. Let go of wanting to have it "my way."

Right now, affirm:

        "I let God be God in my life today."

And let it be so.

TODAY, I AM GRATEFUL FOR: _____

_____

GOD'S DAY 141 — *Thought-Check*

Remember, _____,

(speak your name aloud)

—*to make today a "Thought-Check Day."*

At random times during the day, observe your thoughts and ask yourself:

What are my thoughts right now?
Are they creating peace, or unhappiness?
What will be their consequences,
according to the law of Sowing and Reaping?

Become the "doorman" for your mind. Throw out the self-defeating, troublemaking thoughts and only permit positive, self-affirming ideas to enter.

As a reminder, put small *Thought-Check* signs around the house and at your workplace. Keep one in your wallet or purse, so that you check your thoughts while you are handling your money. Are your thoughts of lack, or of God as your unfailing, unlimited Supply?

Today, remember to let the Christ Mind within you do the thinking!

"Thought-check" your thoughts today!

TODAY, I AM GRATEFUL FOR: _____

GOD'S DAY 142 — Faithful Servants

Remember, _____,
(speak your name aloud)

—to use your faithful servants wisely.

How are you using your body today?
How are you using your hands today?
How are you using your voice?

Your body is a marvelous servant. It was created to be an instrument through which your Higher Self can express love, and create goodness and beauty.

Today, use your body's unique and marvelous abilities to create something beautiful and beneficial. Use it to extend compassion, helpfulness, and generosity.

Use your hands to bless and caress, to build and create.

Use your voice to speak the truth, to encourage and empower, so at the end of the day you can say:

Well done, thou good and faithful servants.

*TODAY, I AM GRATEFUL FOR:*_____

GOD'S DAY 143 — *Take Courage*

Remember, _____,
        (speak your name aloud)

> *"Be strong and of good courage,*
> *do not fear them or be in dread of them;*
> *for it is the Lord your God who goes with you;*
> *he will not fail you or forsake you."*
> —Deuteronomy 31: 6

When you are facing a fearful situation, listen to the inner Voice whispering to you:

> *"Take courage, I am with you.*
> *I will see you safely through this situation."*

No matter what is threatening you—medical prognosis, family troubles, career disasters, legal difficulties—hear that Voice of courage telling you God is with you and will walk you safely through any human difficulty.

Repeat those words to yourself during the day, using your own name:

> *"_____, take courage.*
> *God is seeing you safely through."*

TODAY, I AM GRATEFUL FOR: _____
_____

GOD'S DAY 144 — Step Out In Faith

Remember, _____,
          (speak your name aloud)

          —you have your own life to lead.

Are you leading your own life, or are you merely living in the shadow of someone else?

When you live and work closely with someone, you sometimes find yourself eclipsed by that other person.

You tend to forget your own identity and function as a subordinate. Your own goals and desires are lost or submerged by that stronger person's desires and decisions.

Cooperation and sharing are good, but remember that each of you has a divine creativity that needs to be expressed.

Let go of any guilt about stepping out to express your own creativity. If it is in the highest good of both of you that you work together, so be it. But if the relationship is stifling your own creativity, then it is time to change.

If your desire is of the highest, then Spirit will open a way that will also be in the best interests of both of you.

God is blessing you right now with the courage
to step out and be who you really are!

TODAY, I AM GRATEFUL FOR: _____

_____

GOD'S DAY 145 — *Voice of the Beloved*

Remember, _____,
        (speak your name aloud)

*—in a crowded and noisy room it is difficult to hear
the Voice of your Beloved whispering to you.*

Your daily mind is usually crowded with noisy thoughts and conflicting feelings.

There is no way that you can hear the voice of Spirit speaking to you. There is no way that you can hear the guidance, the protective warnings, and the love that is being spoken to you.

At odd moments through the day take a deep breath and say, *"Thank You, God."*

The noisy corridors of your mind will quiet down and you will hear the Voice of your Beloved.

Take a quiet moment to do that now.

TODAY, I AM GRATEFUL FOR: _____

_____

GOD'S DAY 146 — *Intersection With Destiny*

Remember, _____,
(speak your name aloud)

—you are on a course to intersect with your destiny.

If you are feeling frustrated and unhappy with your life and work, know that there is something "more" to life.

The truth is that your life's journey complete with its detours—has been leading you to the place where you can express the God-given talents you were born to share with the world.

All of your experiences, all of the people that have ever touched your life, have in some way prepared you for your right expression.

Let your prayer be:

Loving Lord, lead me in the path you have laid out for me
before I came into this life experience.

Let me intersect with my destiny,
the work that You would have me do.

Here are the talents You have given me.
Put them to use as You direct.

*TODAY, I AM GRATEFUL FOR:*_____

_____

GOD'S DAY 147 — *Joy*

Remember, _____,
         (speak your name aloud)

    —joy is the unmistakable evidence of the Presence of God.

Whenever you are feeling spontaneous joy, rejoice!

It is your true Self shining through the clouds of your ego.

It is that imprisoned Love leaping forth from your heart.

You can't manufacture true joy. It is not the same as fun or delight. It can only spring forth at the sight of someone you deeply love.

Or in the gift of a resplendent sunrise breaking through the dark clouds.

It is the gift given in meditating deeply on Divine Love when your soul feels that indescribable peace.

Create joy for yourself today by giving yourself away to help someone.

Let your prayer be:

> *Lord, fill me with Your joy that I may pass it on*
> *to others today.*

TODAY, I AM GRATEFUL FOR: _____

_____

GOD'S DAY 148 — Rest

Remember, _____,
         (speak your name aloud)

—to listen for that gentle Voice that speaks continually to you saying:

Come unto me, return to me, and I will give you rest.

As you ask the Voice:

Where will I find you?

The gentle reply comes:

Behind your thoughts and feelings you will find me.
Follow your thoughts and feelings back to your heart
and you will find me there.
At the starting point of your breath you will find me.
Come unto me and rest.

*TODAY, I AM GRATEFUL FOR:*_____

_____

GOD'S DAY 149 — *Master Purpose*

Remember, _____,
(speak your name aloud)

—you are here on Earth to be an instrument
through which the One True Light can shine and express Itself.

You are here to be a prism through which the shaft
of Christ Light can become a rainbow—
shedding Its divine qualities of Love, Peace, Joy, Wisdom,
Creativity, Strength and Power.

Once you know why you are here on Earth,
it changes everything
—how you work, how you love, how you live.

Everything you do is seen against this
Master Purpose
of being an instrument for the Holy Presence
to express Itself through.

Today, be an instrument for the Holy Presence to express through!

TODAY, I AM GRATEFUL FOR: _____

_____

GOD'S DAY 150 — *The Answer*

Remember, _____,
(speak your name aloud)

—always go back to principle!

Just as you must adhere to the principles of mathematics in order to solve any equation, so spiritual principles must be worked in order to solve any of life's problems.

No matter what problem or difficulty is facing you, always go back to principle to solve it.

The one great spiritual Principle is to take your mind off of any problem (which has no power to solve itself) and concentrate on the Answer—the Power of God Omnipresent, and All-Knowing.

Today, in the midst of your problems, remind yourself:

There is only One Presence and One Power in the universe—
God the Good, Omnipotent.

Right now, this very moment, this very hour,
God is setting things right
and arranging my life for my highest good,
and I am grateful.

*TODAY, I AM GRATEFUL FOR:*_____

_____

GOD'S DAY 151 — *Return Ticket*

Remember, _____,
(speak your name aloud)

—life here on Earth is not a one way ticket.

We all arrive here with a return ticket tucked in our back pocket, where it is quickly forgotten.

This trip to the Earth dimension is a spiritual adventure in a foreign land with all the excitement and dangers of a 3D wide-screen adventure movie.

But there always comes a time when the safari adventure into the wilderness is over, and we begin the return journey to our true home.

The difficulty is that we have tripped so far we have forgotten who we really are—spiritual beings. We have come to believe that this foreign land is our home, and we are afraid to board the train for the return journey.

When that time comes for you, know that you will be returning home to a greater love, peace, and joy than you have ever experienced here. So let go and enjoy the return ride.

But for now, just pat the return ticket in your back pocket, relax, remember, and enjoy your safari!

TODAY, I AM GRATEFUL FOR: _____

_____

GOD'S DAY 152 — Health

Remember, _____,
(speak your name aloud)

—love is to the soul as oxygen is to the body—life itself.

Without love your soul withers and dies, and without oxygen your body cannot survive.

Love your body today by taking your body for a walk at a fast pace, breathing deeply as you go.

Do some therapeutic Chi Gong or yoga, both of which are especially beneficial to oxygenate and detoxify the body.

No matter what form of exercise you choose, make sure you do some prolonged forceful breathing to cleanse the toxins and bring fresh oxygen to the cells.

Today, breathe the Holy Breath of Life into your body temple, and give it your love.

Let your prayer be:

I breathe in the Breath of God's Life
and I am renewed and restored.

*TODAY, I AM GRATEFUL FOR:*_____

_____

GOD'S DAY 153 — *Forgiveness*

Remember, _____,
(speak your name aloud)

*—you have mental file cabinets full of old case histories
of people you haven't forgiven—*

—and memories of unhappy experiences, perhaps from several lifetimes. There are files of erroneous beliefs, harsh self-judgments and prejudices that you are still holding on to.

They were all created by false concepts of yourself as a victim or lost, abandoned and separated from your love, support, and protection.

In a time of meditation, visualize yourself going down into the basement of your subconscious where all these files are stored. Bring them up and throw them out to be burned on the trash heap.

Then hold this prayer in your heart:

*I now forgive myself and others of all mistakes,
offenses and misdeeds, forever.*

*Through the power of Christ Love
I now forgive, and I am forgiven.*

*I am free of the past. It no longer has any power to hurt me.
I see myself in a new way—strong, loved, worthy, and free!
Thank You, God!*

TODAY, I AM GRATEFUL FOR: _____

_____

GOD'S DAY 154 — *Give Up to God*

Remember, _____,
(speak your name aloud)

—when you've reached the end of your rope, let go—to God.

When you have reached the end of your strength and try as you may, you can't go on—let God take over.

As you "let go" you fall into the Love of God—the everlasting arms. God will support you and see you through in a way that you cannot even imagine.

Many a healing has taken place after a person has let go in this way. Many a strained relationship has been harmonized after a person stopped trying so hard and let go.

Instead of regarding this as a sign of defeat or giving in to the problem, see it as a giving up to God.

Today, give up to God!

Let your prayer be:

I have done all I can do—there is nothing more I can do,
and so Father, I now let You take over.
I let Your loving will be done in me now.

TODAY, I AM GRATEFUL FOR: _____

_____

GOD'S DAY 155 — *Success*

Remember, _____,
　　　　　(speak your name aloud)

　　　　　—never underestimate the power of one.

　　　One match, one candle, one right word spoken at the right time can save a life. One divine idea can start a new business or community project.

　　　If a single dandelion can succeed in its great idea to be "fruitful and multiply" right in the middle of your green lawn, then surely you can succeed in seeing your soul's sincerest desires come true!

　　　It is the nature of all things to grow and expand, and it is in your basic nature to grow and express in new ways that are uniquely yours.

　　　Stop selling yourself short! Your dreams, your creative ideas may be just what the world and the marketplace needs and is waiting for.

　　　Dare to step out on faith, take God as your Partner, and begin today!

　　　Let your prayer be:

Lord, I am ready for a new beginning!
Give me the strength, wisdom and resources
to bring my dreams—and Yours through me—into fruition!

TODAY, I AM GRATEFUL FOR: _____

_____

GOD'S DAY 156 — *Follow Your Dreams*

Remember, _____,
(speak your name aloud)

—to come up higher today.

Come up higher to live the Truth you know.

Raise your sights today. Aim at the highest goal of your hearts desire.

That yearning you feel, that vague discontent with how things are for you now, that whisper that there is something yet more—that is the Lord of your being, your Higher Self prompting you to follow your dreams.

Follow your highest aspirations that you have always wanted to be and do, but never dared.

Close your eyes now.

Ask: *What is the deepest yearning of my heart?*

Scan your deepest desires.

Come up past the lower goals to the higher one

with the light around it. That is what you came here to do.

Ask: *What is the first step towards reaching it?*

Take that step today. Fall in step with the Lord.

Stride together toward that high goal.

*TODAY, I AM GRATEFUL FOR:*_____

_____

GOD'S DAY 157 — Angel Power

Remember, _____,
          (speak your name aloud)

          —*to put your Angel Power to work!*

Each of the people in your life has a Christ Angel, and so do you. It is the Angel of God's Presence ever with you as your higher Self. It is the Power of God ever standing ready to help.

When you are praying for someone—a child, or a family member—try writing a spiritual "letter" to their Angel asking for help.

If you are having difficulty with someone, write a spiritual "letter" to their Angel asking for harmony and understanding to be established. By addressing their Angel you will be contacting the highest and best in them, and bypassing their outer personality that is in conflict with yours.

Instead of your two egos clashing, it will be your two Angels finding common ground on a higher level.

In your meditation time now, write that "letter."

Keep it to read and pray with every day for that person.

Put your Angel Power to work today!

TODAY, I AM GRATEFUL FOR: _____

Prayer to Christ Angel
(praying for others)

Beloved Christ, Angel of (name),
True and Rightful Self,
I call You forth.
I bless You and see You magnified in _____.
Let the outer become as the Inner.

Oh, Christ, Thou Son of God—
Live Your life in _____
until there is only You.
Be made flesh in _____
until You shine resurrected in every cell of his body.

Live Your peace in _____
until there is no more fear and only You.
Live Your love in _____
until there is no more hurt and only You.
Live Your faith in _____
until there is no more self-doubt and only the certainty
of Your love.
Lift his heart with Your hope.

Do Your Will in _____
until there is no will but Yours.
Shine now Your Light in _____
until there is no more darkness, and only Your Light
in every corner of his consciousness.
Shine now Your love through _____

until there is only joy shining in his eyes—
—until Your eyes are his and his Yours—
and the two become one, and there is only You.
O, Christ, Thou Son of God, I thank You.

Oh, Divine Mother, Holy Comforter, Healer, and Nurturer,
—enfold _____ now in Your Love.
Encourage and strengthen him.
Give him Hope and Light to follow his bliss—
his True Purpose in life.
Thank You. Amen

GOD'S DAY 158 — The Way Up

Remember, _____,
(speak your name aloud)

—the way out of your difficulties,
the way through the tangled situation—is the way UP!

Lift up your inner eye to the wisdom, power, and protection of God, who opens ways where to human sense there appears no way.

Acknowledge that Inner Power in all your ways and let it direct your path.

Let this be your prayer today:

God is opening new doors of deliverance for me now.
I am loved and I am safe.
I am protected and provided for in all my ways,
and I am grateful!
Thank You, God!

*TODAY, I AM GRATEFUL FOR:*_____

_____

GOD'S DAY 159 — *Pour Off the Wax*

Remember, _____,
(speak your name aloud)

—to get rid of the wax in your life.

If you have ever used a votive candle during your meditation time, you may have noticed that after burning for awhile, the flame begins to drown in its own molten wax.

If you pour off the wax, and relight the wick, the flame will burn bright and steady again.

Our lives are like that candle—too much wax.

Ask yourself:

Are my soul's light, joy, and creativity, drowning in a buildup of mental, emotional and material wax?

Get rid of the wax—the material junk in your closets and garage. More importantly—get rid of the resentments, regrets, self-blame and self-doubts that your soul is drowning in.

In your quiet time now, visualize yourself letting go of that mental and emotional wax.

Today, hold this thought:

Today, I get rid of the wax,
and let my Inner Light shine!

TODAY, I AM GRATEFUL FOR: _____

GOD'S DAY 160 — Seed Thoughts

Remember, _____,
(speak your name aloud)

Grow no weeds!

Post these words on your mirror to remind yourself to stay away from negative thinking.

What you continually think about comes true as the harvest in your daily life— for better or for worse.

All of the old habits and self-defeating thoughts continue to reproduce themselves unless they are weeded out and replaced with positive self-affirming ones.

Today, observe your thoughts closely during the day. Do not let any negative seeds take root in the garden of your mind. Weed out the noxious weeds of fear, self-doubt, and regret.

Replace them with seed thoughts of courage, confidence, and serenity.

In your quiet time now, meditate on this idea:

I plant the garden of my mind with seeds of God's courage, confidence, and peace.

TODAY, I AM GRATEFUL FOR: _____

_____

GOD'S DAY 161 — *Calm Observer*

Remember, _____,
(speak your name aloud)

—to be a train watcher today.

Stop the continuous thought trains rolling through your mind.

Become the detached observer. Step back and let the train of thoughts pass by, as you would watch a freight train passing by at a railroad crossing.

Create a positive train of thoughts by choosing a God-thought to be the engine pulling a new train of thoughts.

For a Health engine, use:

> *The Life of God is strong within me,*
> *healing and restoring me right now.*

For a Prosperity engine, use;

> *God's ever-present Supply is providing for me*
> *in every way today.*

For a Protection engine, use:

> *God is my shield and my defender.*

Meditate on the Thought Engine that is most powerful for you today.

TODAY, I AM GRATEFUL FOR: _____

_____

GOD'S DAY 162 — Soul-Quakes

Remember, _____,

>   (speak your name aloud)

>   *—to let nothing disturb you.*

In the midst of the outer world's turmoil and violence, let nothing disturb you. In the midst of your inner world's unrest, let nothing disturb you.

Know that in the midst of these inner "soul-quakes" that threaten to shake the very ground of your being— God's Presence is ever with you.

St. Teresa of Avila's beautiful prayer is most strengthening at this time:

> *"Let nothing disturb you, naught fright you ever.*
> *All things are changing, God changes never!"*

Today in your meditation, hold to this prayer as soul-shaking changes happen all around you.

Know that as you hold firm, something better than you can presently imagine will come out of all the chaos and turmoil. New good, now unseen, will come forth.

Today, let nothing disturb You.

*TODAY, I AM GRATEFUL FOR:*_____

GOD'S DAY 163 — You Are Loved

Remember, _____,
　　　　　　(speak your name aloud)

　—to ask: *What is it that I forgot to remember?*

I forgot to remember that I am loved.

I forgot to remember to love myself.

I forgot to remember to stop judging myself.

I forgot to remember to free myself from the bonds

of self-imposed limitations.

I forgot to_____

I forgot to_____

Remember, a rose in every stage of its blossoming, is perfect. So you are to love yourself in every stage of your soul's unfolding.

The most important thing to remember is—

I am loved, and I am worth loving.

And I am an instrument of God's Love.

Today, remember you are loved!

TODAY, I AM GRATEFUL FOR: _____

_____

GOD'S DAY 164 — *Strong and Capable*

Remember, _____,
(speak your name aloud)

—yesterday you asked the question:

What is it that I forgot to remember?

Today, ask:

What do I need to forget?

I need to forget all my imagined faults and weaknesses—as well as all imagined hurts and mistakes. (Forget and release them; and cease dwelling on them)

I need to forget about wasted opportunities.

Everything that we have experienced can be used for our growth —even seeming delays and side journeys. We need to trust God and not resist the learning.

I need to forget the imprints, untruths, and limitations that others have put on me.

As a child, you may have been told that you would never amount to anything, or that you were too much this or that. Your young mind was so impressionable. You accepted as true everything that adults said about you.

Today, forget your self-doubts and what others say, and remember you are a strong, capable, and worth loving!

*TODAY, I AM GRATEFUL FOR:*_____

GOD'S DAY 165 — *Loosen Up*

Remember, _____,
(speak your name aloud)

—to loosen up and let God take over.

If you have been praying 'hard" for a physical healing, a business deal, a relationship, or any other special desire—it is best to simply surrender your anxiety to your Higher Power.

Sometimes we hang on to a desired result so tightly that we choke it to death. Our anxiety acts like a tourniquet that restricts the flow of God's good. We need to loosen up and let God take care of the outcome.

Let your prayer be:

"Loving Spirit, here is my desire.
I surrender it totally to you.

Let it be done according to your Will, not mine,
for the highest good of all concerned.
Thank You!

Relax, and let the peace of God fill your heart and mind now. Your good will come to you in the right way and at the right time.

TODAY, I AM GRATEFUL FOR: _____

_____

GOD'S DAY 166 — *Extract the Blessing*

Remember, _____,
           (speak your name aloud)

     —be done with useless unnecessary suffering.

There are two kinds of suffering. The first is the useless, unnecessary suffering you create for yourself when you insist on having your way in matters and you can't have it. It is the suffering that comes from continuing to blame yourself or another for your situation.

It is the suffering you experience when you resist, resent and refuse to give your troubles to God. The longer you resist, the longer you suffer.

Extract the blessing from the suffering by ceasing to be willful. Instead ask:

     What soul lesson can I gain from this experience?
     How can I convert this suffering to my benefit?

Make the suffering work for your soul's benefit by using it to deepen your connection with God.

Let the experience show you what is really important in life and what is really of lasting value.

Let your prayer be:

     Lord, here is my suffering. I give it to you.
     Show me the blessing in it.
     Transform it with your love.

*TODAY, I AM GRATEFUL FOR:*_____

GOD'S DAY 167 — *Play*

Remember, _____,
          (speak your name aloud)

            —to play more and fret less.

A bumper sticker on a car driven by what looked to be a retired, lively, grandmotherly person, read:

    Don't bother me. I'm living Happily Ever After!

How do we live Happily Ever After? We begin to love what we are doing at the moment we are doing it. We see the lighter side of life. We laugh at ourselves more. We play more, and fret less. We reach out and enjoy the people in our daily life more.

And we remind ourselves that there is nothing to fear about tomorrow, for God is already there. And God is laughing!

Today, remember to play more, and fret less…live Happily Ever After!

TODAY, I AM GRATEFUL FOR: _____

_____

GOD'S DAY 168 — Eyes of Love

Remember, _____,
                   (speak your name aloud)

—the world you look out upon is only the world of effects.
You see not the Cause.

You see the leaves on the trees moving and dancing, but you see not the wind that makes them dance.

You see the smile on the faces of your loved ones, but you see not the love in their hearts that makes them smile.

Today, look at your world with the eyes of love, and you will see the Unseen beyond the seen. You will see as God sees—all things bright and beautiful.

Look upon yourself and smile. You are God's beloved!

Let your prayer be:

Today, I look with eyes of love upon my world.

*TODAY, I AM GRATEFUL FOR:*_____
_____

GOD'S DAY 169 — *Multidimensional Being*

Remember, _____,

      (speak your name aloud)

   —you are so much greater than you appear to be!

You are a multidimensional being—capable of being everywhere and everywhen.

Close your eyes and concentrate on your breathing and being inside your body. Just be aware of your physical self. Feel its size, its energy. Feel yourself being inside your skin.

Still with your eyes closed sense the room around you—its size, its energy. Let your antennas sense the objects and atmosphere.

Now transport yourself mentally to be with a family member. Stand next to them in your mind and talk to them. Now be with a loved one in the spirit dimension. Be with them in spirit. They are only a thought away.

Now, time travel back to your childhood home. Be there as your child self, feel your feelings, your fears, your joys…now travel forward in time to tomorrow.

Now become one with Nature—a cloud, a soaring eagle, a mighty redwood. Feel one with it. Be it. You are part of the Allness of God, one with all life.

You have been everywhere and everywhen, past, present and future. You are a multidimensional being with infinite possibilities! Today, be your unlimited Self, and be all that you can be!

TODAY, I AM GRATEFUL FOR: _____

_____

GOD'S DAY 170 — Be Mindful

Remember, _____,

(speak your name aloud)

—to stay in the present moment.

Our thoughts have a bad habit of racing ahead into the future—things to be done, children to be picked up, or the next appointment to be met.

Our minds are always way out ahead of our body, leaving it to take care of itself the best it can. It is no wonder our body is neglected and gets into accidents.

Before you turn the key in the ignition, your mind has already sped far ahead, and you are barely conscious of backing out of the garage.

Be mindful as you climb into your car today.

Remind yourself:

"Right here, right now God is in charge."

Let it ground you to the present moment and the task at hand.

*TODAY, I AM GRATEFUL FOR:*_____

GOD'S DAY 171 — *Hidden Gifts*

Remember, _____,
                    (speak your name aloud)

   —every change comes to you with a gift in its hands.

   Unfortunately, when you hold a negative attitude toward it, the gift appears to be wrapped in unattractive paper. You don't want to open it.

   Remember, change is the only way that your Higher Power can possibly move you into new good. You have to let go of the old good, so you can take hold of the new good God has for you.

   Do you have an unattractive change in your life right now?

   In your quiet time now, ask God to show you the gift hidden in the unattractive wrapping paper.

   Let your prayer be:

   Lord, show me the gift hidden in this change.

TODAY, I AM GRATEFUL FOR: _____

GOD'S DAY 172 — Healing Hands

Remember, _____,
     (speak your name aloud)

    *—the power to heal is in
    your own hands.*

Open your heart to God's love and
let it flow through your hands to bless
and to heal.

Concentrate on God's Love flowing through you and you
will feel the energy radiating from your palms.

In your meditation and prayer time now, think of a loved
one in need of healing.

Go to them in your imagination and lay your hands gently
upon them. Ask God to use you as an instrument for God to heal
through. Feel God's healing Love flowing through your hands
to bless them.

Let your prayer be:

    *Here are my hands, Lord.
    Use them.*

TODAY, I AM GRATEFUL FOR: _____

_____

GOD'S DAY 173 — *One Candle*

Remember, _____,
　　　　　(speak your name aloud)

—one person holding high thoughts of God's Love
can counteract the negative consciousness
of several hundred people.
You have that power!

You are the one candle that can light the darkness, and all the darkness in the world cannot overcome it. You are the light of your world!

Your one prayer knowing that God's love is greater, your one prayer sending forth God's Love to a person in darkness—will dispel their fear and anger.

Today, light one candle—send forth one prayer to someone who is in the darkness of fear or despair.

Let your prayer for them be:

The Light of Christ within you lights your way out
of darkness and despair.
Follow the light to safety.

TODAY, I AM GRATEFUL FOR: _____

_____

GOD'S DAY 174 — Return Home

Remember, _____,
         (speak your name aloud)

—you are the prodigal.
Awaken and return to the Father.

You have been journeying in the far country of fear and the world of appearances. You have lost your way in the world of materialism and wasted your precious inheritance. Awaken and return home.

You have journeyed so far that you have forgotten who you are—the beloved child of an infinitely loving Father.

Return inward now in prayer to your heavenly Father.

Close your eyes. Take a deep breath.

The door of your Father's house stands open in welcome. Enter into the Light and rest there.

You are home.

Father, I have come home.
Thank You for Your love.
Thank You for never giving up on me.

*TODAY, I AM GRATEFUL FOR:*_____

GOD'S DAY 175 — *Never Too Late*

Remember, _____,
(speak your name aloud)

—it is always later than you think,
but you have all the time you need!

It is never too late to love!

It is never too late to forgive.

It is never too late to open yourself to be an instrument for Spirit to work through.

It is never too late to make a new beginning.

It makes no difference where you are, or how dark or limited the conditions you live under.

You have the power to turn your thoughts to God and declare:

Right now, this very moment I make a new beginning!

Right now, this very day, I open myself
to be an instrument for God to work through!

Here I am. Lord, use me now!

Today, make that new beginning—with God!

TODAY, I AM GRATEFUL FOR: _____

_____

GOD'S DAY 176 — Stay Awake

Remember, _____,
(speak your name aloud)

—to stay awake.

This Earth trip your soul is experiencing right now is a sleepy one—a dream state.

It is a struggle to stay awake and remember who you truly are—a Light being, and where you come from—the realms of glory.

It is so easy to fall back asleep and dream that you are some character in an adventure movie that is both comic and horrifying.

Today, wake up and remember that you are a powerful spiritual being, in charge of your own destiny.

Peace, Light, and Love is what I am.

TODAY, I AM GRATEFUL FOR:_____

_____

GOD'S DAY 177 — *Transformed*

Remember, _____,

(speak your name aloud)

—you are not that person anymore!

You do not have to justify or defend, or identify with old limited personality traits or career roles anymore.

Some people may tend to hold you to being the way you used to be. They categorize or even stigmatize you as being a certain way—not giving you the freedom to change.

But you have moved on, even within the role itself, you have grown. You no longer have to be captive of it. You are a master of it.

Close your eyes, take a deep breath and step out of the old role, old label.

See yourself in a higher way—standing free, wise, and capable.

For that is what you truly are!

Today I see myself as God created me to be
—strong, capable, courageous, and loving!

TODAY, I AM GRATEFUL FOR: _____

_____

GOD'S DAY 178 — Share Your Love

Remember, _____,
(speak your name aloud)

—life is short—don't waste it on loveless trivialities.

Only that which is done in love will last.

Only that which has beauty in it will last.

Life is short—you came to be an instrument, an agent of God's Love. Find a way to express that Love today. Share it and give it away.

Remember, love is the only thing that multiplies itself when you give it away.

In your quiet time now, ask the Giver of all Life and Love how you can share that Light and Love and Goodwill today.

Ask to be shown a way to give it in a way that will be most meaningful to those receiving it.

Let your prayer be:

Lord, show me the way to express Your love today.

*TODAY, I AM GRATEFUL FOR:*_____

GOD'S DAY 179 — *Programmed for Success*

Remember, _____,
(speak your name aloud)

Garbage in, garbage out.

Computers mindlessly print out data regardless of whether or not that data is erroneous. Yet the computer itself is not to blame, it simply accepts the data that you enter into it.

The same is true of your mind—like a computer, it gives you a printout of whatever you have programmed into it—for better or for worse.

Your life is a printout of the personal beliefs you have programmed into it, as well as the programming installed by your family, society, and the TV/media.

There is a lot of garbage in there, and it is giving you a bad printout in terms of the habits, people, and experiences you are drawing to yourself.

Today, ask your Higher Power, the Master Programmer— to get rid of the viruses and the mental and emotional garbage, and reinstall the original programming placed in you by your Creator.

Let your prayer be:

*"Lord, clear out my old mental and emotional garbage.
Think your thoughts through me, live through me,
love through me, do Thou Thy will in me."*

TODAY, I AM GRATEFUL FOR: _____

GOD'S DAY *180* — *Promptings*

Remember, _____,
(speak your name aloud)

—to follow your promptings.

Your human intellect likes to think in 1—2—3 logical, linear steps. This is fine, but it doesn't leave any openings for divine synchronicity to come into play.

When you follow your intuition you enjoy chance encounters with unexpected blessings. You discover things long lost or mislaid.

You are prompted to turn down streets you had not planned and afterwards find out that you had missed a major traffic accident.

You catch a different commuter train than usual and meet someone who turns out to be just the person you needed to meet at that particular time in your life.

Be ready to break out of the logical sequence that you have planned for your day. Follow your promptings.

You will know whether or not they are right by the feeling of lightness and peace they give you. If the feeling is heavy or dark, it is not right for you. God's promptings always bring a blessing.

Declare:

Today, I go with the flow of divine synchronicity!

*TODAY, I AM GRATEFUL FOR:*_____

GOD'S DAY 181 — God's Hands

Remember, _____,
(speak your name aloud)

—the mind and the hand are one.

The hand is the executive power of the mind carrying out the intentions of the mind that directs it.

The question is—which mind is directing your hands…your lower mind or your Higher Mind?

Would God's hands feed the body toxic food or drink, or drugs? Would God's hands do harm or violence?

During your daily activities at home or at work remind yourself:

These are God's hands shaking hands on a business deal..
These are God's hands driving.
These are God's hands making supper—
it will be a better supper because of that thought.
These are God's hands holding God's child.
These are Gods hands changing the diapers on another one
of God's creations.
These are God's hands healing.
These are God's hands building and crafting.

Put a rubber band on your wrist today, to remind yourself this is God's hand. Start your day with this prayer:

Beloved Lord within,
here are your hands.
What do you want to do with them today?

TODAY, I AM GRATEFUL FOR: _____

GOD'S DAY 182 — *Windows of the Soul*

Remember, _____,
(speak your name aloud)

—be a dream-watcher.

Dreams are the windows of the soul, through which you can peer into the many layers of yourself.

Spirit will often use dreams to reach you when your mind is blocked by worry and not open to guidance.

In your prayers before sleeping, ask to be instructed though your dreams. Keep a notebook by your bedside. Watch for recurring dreams for they always have an important message that is trying to get through to you.

Write the dream down immediately, before it slips away from you upon fully awakening. Begin by describing the dream in detail and be sure to describe the feelings you felt in the dream.

Then dialogue with its major characters, objects and events. Ask of each one,

*"What or whom do you represent in me,
and what message do you have for me?"*

You will get surprising answers, especially if you write the answers with your non-dominant hand to access your right brain.

Pleasant dreams!

*TODAY, I AM GRATEFUL FOR:*_____

GOD'S DAY 183 — *Beauty All around You*

Remember, _____,
(speak your name aloud)

—everything has beauty, but few see it.

Can you see the beauty in the people and the everyday things around you?

In this world there are so many delights to behold, yet we miss so many of them.

Today, pay attention to detail—not only in the things around you, but also in the people.

Watch how *a smile* breaks on the face of an acquaintance or loved one.

See *the twinkle* in a child's eyes —or a grown-up's for that matter!

Behold *the grace* with which people and animals move. Be aware of the red bird perched on the tree limb, and hear its song.

Look closely at your world, for everything has beauty. May you have the inner vision to appreciate it!

Let your prayer be:

Lord, make me aware of the beauty of Your world today.

TODAY, I AM GRATEFUL FOR: _____

GOD'S DAY 184 — *Calling Home*

Remember, _____,
> (speak your name aloud)

> *—you are here to heal your sense of separation.*
> *Get on with it.*

Get on with healing your sense of being far away from home—far away from safety, far away from love, far away from the good you so passionately desire. Far away from that place of Peace you yearn for.

Get on with healing that yearning by "calling home" in your meditation now.

Get back in touch with the Father within who is waiting to hear from you.

You have been the prodigal too long.

Let your prayer be:

> *Loving Father, here I am on your doorstep.*
> *Take me into your warm embrace.*

*TODAY, I AM GRATEFUL FOR:*_____

GOD'S DAY 185 — *Nature Break*

Remember, _____,
> (speak your name aloud)

> *—to take a nature break today.*

Is there a beautiful river nearby, or a quiet country stream, perhaps with a gentle waterfall? Go there, if only in your mind.

Sit by the quiet running waters and feel your kinship with ancient streams running through your veins.

You and the stream are part of the great Mother ocean.

Imagine the stream to be the waters of God's healing love.

Reach into the dark corners of your heart and pull out any pain, or fear that has been troubling you. and drop it into the healing waters to be dissolved by that Love. Reach in again and again until all pain has been dropped into the cleansing waters.

Let nature do her healing work in you today.

*TODAY, I AM GRATEFUL FOR:*_____

_____

GOD'S DAY 186 — *Patience*

Remember, _____,
> (speak your name aloud)

> —*be patient.*

Be like the surfer at the beach waiting patiently on his surfboard for that perfect wave to ride. He floats easily, enjoying the view, until the wave rises behind him and swoops him joyously forward on its foaming crest.

Be like the great artists and authors waiting for the wave of inspiration to carry them forward.

There is an ebb and flow of God's opportunities—an ebb and flow to miracles and the so-called "lucky breaks" in life.

Whatever you are striving for now, cease striving. Give it to God.

Be patient and enjoy the view of what life has to offer. Your own shall come to you.

> *Spirit, patiently I wait.*
> *Patiently I rest in you.*

> *In your divine timing rise up within me*
> *and sweep me along on your mighty wave of opportunity!.*

TODAY, I AM GRATEFUL FOR: _____

_____

GOD'S DAY 187 — *Live In Lover*

Remember, _____,

(speak your name aloud)

—you have a "live-in-lover!"

God loves you with an everlasting love, and lives right in your heart!

This is the great mystery of the indwelling Presence!

You have a *"live-in-healer"* too—a healing Presence that is continually at work renewing and restoring you to your original strength and wholeness.

And you have a *"live-in-friend,"* a *"live-in counselor,"* and a *"live-in banker"* as well!

Take time now in your meditation to get in touch with this "live-in' Presence.

You who dwells within me—thank You!
You who loves me, and befriends me—thank You!
You who protects me and provides for me—thank You!
I rest in Your Presence now, and all is well.

*TODAY, I AM GRATEFUL FOR:*_____

_____

GOD'S DAY 188 — *Springboards*

Remember, _____,
　　　　　　(speak your name aloud)

　—to ask yourself these important questions today.

　Dialogue with them in your quiet time now.

What am I here for?
What is the reason for my being?

For what purpose did my soul choose to incarnate,
and why at this particular time?

Who was I supposed to meet, and for what reason
did our lives intersect?

What soul lessons did we have to learn from each other?

　Let these be springboards for discovering yourself and your true path, today.

TODAY, I AM GRATEFUL FOR: _____

_____

GOD'S DAY 189 — Inner Ideal

Remember, _____,
               (speak your name aloud)

—to let go of regrets about so-called mistakes of the past.

There really is no such thing as a mistake. Rather, every experience is a learning opportunity.

We have an inner ideal, a picture of ourselves as we want to be. When we fall short of that inner picture, we say we made a mistake. The old Greek word for "sin" is an archery term meaning to miss the mark.

What do you do when you make a mistake—do you waste time regretting it? Your time is better spent in taking a new look at your inner picture and trying again to measure up to it in your outer life.

Each time you aim at what you desire to be, you automatically draw closer to the mark.

Leave all so-called mistakes behind. They are past. Release them.

In your meditation, hold the thought:

"Lord, thank you for this new day—
a day to more closely live my inner ideal.
Thank you for helping me to be all that I can be!

TODAY, I AM GRATEFUL FOR: _____

GOD'S DAY 190 — *Be Willing*

Remember, _____,
   (speak your name aloud)

   —*to set your intention for transformation.*

Every step of progress that you make individually, you also make for all humanity.

You are not striving alone. You are lifted up by the efforts of every other person on Earth, just as they are lifted up by your efforts. Our global spiritual transformation rides on the wave of our combined efforts.

In your quiet time today, set your intention with this thought:

*Lord, I am willing to be transformed
into what you desire me to be.*

I am willing to be transformed by Thy Love.

Let Thy Will be done in and through me now.

That is the commitment God is waiting to hear from you. As soon as you make that commitment, everything will converge and coordinate to make it happen for you.

Just be willing.

TODAY, I AM GRATEFUL FOR: _____

_____

GOD'S DAY 191 — Excess Baggage

Remember, _____,
> (speak your name aloud)

> *—you are just passing through this lifetime,*
> *you don't need a lot of baggage to burden you.*

Get rid of the excess—the baggage and "naggage" of past unhappy memories. Let them go. Don't continue to carry them into the present. Give them to God.

Get rid of the excess—the burdensome soul-stifling relationships. Let them go. Forgive the people involved and release them to their good.

Get rid of the excess—the possessions that possess you with their heavy responsibilities and upkeep. Let them go.

Take a quiet moment now to close your eyes, and visualize letting go of your excess baggage.

Start with your fears and doubts, then move on to old unhappy memories, then, soul-stifling relationships.

Finally mentally scan your home and personal possessions, and see yourself letting go of the excess.

Declare:

> *I travel light through life!*
> *I free up my soul and let it soar with joy!*
> *Lighter in mind, heart, and affairs,*
> *I move forward on the wonderful journey ahead of me!*

*TODAY, I AM GRATEFUL FOR:*_____

_____

GOD'S DAY 192 — *You Are A Blessing*

Remember, _____,
            (speak your name aloud)

—you are an idea in the Mind of God—
an expression of love in the Heart of God.

You cannot possibly conceive of how much God loves you and desires to express through you today.

You are the only one at this moment that can express God's idea in precisely the right way today. You are the only one in the right place and the right circumstances to accomplish what God desires to accomplish today. That is why the idea came to you, and not someone else.

In your quiet time listen for the idea God desires to express through you.

It will have something to do with creating. It will have something to do with loving someone, or reaching out to help someone, or bringing peace to a situation. It will have something to do with beauty. It will have something to do with making you to be a blessing to the world today.

Listen, and say, *Yes, Lord, I will.*

Remember:

I am an idea in the Mind of God,
I am an expression of love in the Heart of God.
I let that divine idea express itself through me now.

TODAY, I AM GRATEFUL FOR: _____

_____

GOD'S DAY 193 — The Breath of Life

Remember, _____,
　　　　　　(speak your name aloud)

—when you breathe all life breathes with you,
for you are all one breath.

The air you breathe today was brought by the west wind from the far Pacific, or Hawaii, or the jet stream carrying it down from Canada.

The air you breathe in now has been breathed out by a baby in Afghanistan, or perhaps a mountain climber in Tibet.

The air you breathed out last week will be carried by the wind to be breathed in by a great blue whale surfacing in the Pacific, or an elephant working the teak forests of Burma.

The wind makes us one with all the air-breathing creatures on Earth.

The oxygen you breathe in now has come perhaps from the trees of the great rain forests of Brazil, and the carbon dioxide you breathe out has nourished the plants growing on your windowsill.

And the prayers you breathe out are felt by creatures all over this beautiful blue planet.

Breathe out a prayer blessing today.

*TODAY, I AM GRATEFUL FOR:*_____

_____

GOD'S DAY 194 — *Loving Presence*

Remember, _____,
(speak your name aloud)

—someone loves you.

It may be another person, but most assuredly it is that loving Spirit, that Presence of the Holy One who is ever with you—watching over you awake or asleep.

When you feel most alone, that Loving Presence never stops loving you. No matter what you have done, no matter how mired in despair you seem to be, that Love waits for you, saying:

Come unto me. Return to me.

In your meditation now, take time to return to that Love that waits for you at the center of your heart.

Take time to say:

Thank You, Lord, for Your Love.

TODAY, I AM GRATEFUL FOR: _____

_____

GOD'S DAY 195 — *Mindfulness*

Remember, _____,
(speak your name aloud)

> *—to really taste your food today.*
> *Make a mindful meditation of it today.*

Be really mindful of every bite. Bless the nourishing life within it.

Taste its texture, savor its flavor. Smell its aroma.

Take a moment to think of where it came from.

Take a moment to thank those who labored to grow it, and all the hands that brought it to your table.

It is a small thing to do, but it will put you in touch with the Source of all nourishment, body, and soul, alike.

> *Today, be mindful, in all the small things of life.*
> *Be aware of how blessed you are.*

*TODAY, I AM GRATEFUL FOR:*_____

_____

GOD'S DAY 196 — *Virtual Reality*

Remember, _____,
(speak your name aloud)

—what you see is what you get.

What is the good that you'd love to see come into your life today? What deep earnest desire would you love to see come true?

Get a clear picture of it in your mind right now. Don't worry about the "how" of it— leave that to God. Simply get a strong image of it and plant that desire-seed in the garden of your subconscious and start it growing. Water it with your love, and give it the sunshine of your faith.

Next, gain the feeling of joy that you would feel if your desire were already accomplished. How would you feel? Make that feeling real. Act as if you already have it. Make it virtual reality in your mind and heart right here and now— not in the future. Now is the Moment of Power

Jesus said: *"…. Whatever you ask for in prayer, believe that you have received it, and it will be yours."* (Mark 11:24)

Finally, give thanks for it:

Thank you, Father,
that I have already received this blessing
according to your will for my highest good.
I am so grateful!

TODAY, I AM GRATEFUL FOR: _____

_____

GOD'S DAY 197 — *Storms of Life*

Remember, _____,
         (speak your name aloud)

—after the storm comes the rainbow.

In the desert southwest a thunderstorm lashes a high mesa with lightning and driving torrents of rain.

After the storm the black sky clears to a beautiful rainbow and new flowers sprang forth from the desert floor—birthed by the rain.

When the storms of life batter you, stand undaunted, knowing that rainbows of new blessings and new opportunities will spring forth in their wake.

Every change, even those that seem so traumatic— hide rainbows in them.

Today, stand fast in your faith in the midst of the storm, and look for the rainbow.

It is God's promise of blessings to you!

Lord, help me to stand fast in faith in the storms of life.

Help me to know that you will bring new blessings and rainbows of opportunities in their wake.

TODAY, I AM GRATEFUL FOR: _____

GOD'S DAY 198 — *Mutual Support System*

Remember, _____,
(speak your name aloud)

—you were created to function as part of a
Universal Mutual Support System.

There is no need for you to feel discouraged, for the truth is that you have been endowed with unique talents, resources and energies that the world needs.

For every demand, Infinite Intelligence has also created the right supply. You are part of that supply, as well as part of the demand. Thus you are automatically guaranteed a role to play for you are part of the System.

If you have not yet aligned yourself with the System and have been trying to function on your own, not only are you paddling against the current, but you are not fulfilling your rightful role in the System.

As you fulfill that role, the things you need for living on this Earth plane are also provided for you through the System.

To find your role, you need only to be willing to serve, ask for guidance from the Creator of the System, and remove the blocks to the fulfilling of your role. Your self-empowerment lies in staying tuned to this Source—for from it flows all that you will ever need to succeed in life.

Remember:

I am part of a universal mutual support system.
My every need is taken care of.

TODAY, I AM GRATEFUL FOR: _____

GOD'S DAY 199 — *Senior Partner*

Remember, _____,
(speak your name aloud)

*—work in the twenty-first century is not something you do,
it is something that is done through you.*

It is an *inside job.* You shift from working by the "sweat of your brow" (your own limited intellect,) to tuning into the Higher Wisdom of your Inner Partner.

This Inner Partner will not only lead you to your right work, but It will accomplish that work through you as well, if you will but cooperate.

Make a commitment now to join into partnership with that Creative Intelligence today. Commit to listening daily to that Senior Partner for counsel and direction.

I, _____, hereby commit to enter into partnership with the Creative Intelligence, also known as Inner Partner or Senior Partner—within me.

I hereby commit to listening daily to my Senior Partner for counsel and direction.

I hereby dedicate myself, my loyalty, my time and my energies to this Partnership.

In return, it is understood and agreed that the Senior Partner shall render unto me an equivalent for my dedication, in peace of mind, wisdom, prospering ideas and abundant resources to make this Partnership a success.

In thanksgiving and gratitude to my Partner,

Signed _____

*Date*_____

TODAY, I AM GRATEFUL FOR:_____

_____

Prayer For Right Expression

Holy Spirit,
I now let go of fear and doubt,
and take hold of the divine idea that there is Good
for me and I am being directed to that Good right now.

I give thanks that You are already preparing
the right new work for my highest good,
and that You are bringing this about in the right way,
at the right time, in the right place.

I give thanks that in this right new work
I will be abundantly prospered in the right way—
not only financially, but also in the inner satisfaction
I will be making the best use of the talents and abilities
that You have given me to help and serve others.

I ask and give thanks in the full assurance
that this or something better is now being provided—
not according to my will, but in accordance with
Thy loving wonderful Will for my highest Good.

My Right Work is opening to me now!

Trusting and resting,
I place myself and all my affairs
in Thy loving care.

Thank You, Spirit.

God is my Partner, I cannot fail!
God is my Partner, together we succeed!

GOD'S DAY 200 — *Inner Abundance*

Remember, _____,
(speak your name aloud)

—the grass is not always greener on the other side.

Have you ever seen a cow that has poked her head through a hole in a barbed wire fence to nibble the grass on the other side?

Though there are acres of good grazing land in her own field, she just had to have the grass beyond the fence—which obviously is the same as the grass right under her feet! It is a perfect example of *"The grass is always greener on the other side."*

We are frequently like that cow—discontented with where we are and with what we have. We think that somewhere outside is our utopia!

Let's awaken to the Truth and realize that *what we need is right where we are!*

Let your prayer be:

Right where I am,
I know God is my instant, constant, unfailing Supply.

Right where I am,
I live in a field of God's Abundance.
Thank You, God!

*TODAY, I AM GRATEFUL FOR:*_____

GOD'S DAY 201 — *Breaking Out of Your Shell*

Remember, _____,
        (speak your name aloud)

*—when you feel most closed in
        and most confined,*
*it may be Life's way of telling you that it's time
        to break out of your shell into new Good!*

Picture an eggshell, lying cracked open and empty. Standing in the middle is a wide-eyed chick, in stunned disbelief, shouting, *"OH, WOW! PARADIGM SHIFT!"*

An egg is the perfect environment for the little being developing inside of it. But as that being grows, its surroundings become so confined that the only way to live is to break out of the shell. So the chick pecks its way out, and Wham! A whole new world to explore!

Today dare to "break out" of your old comfort and security shell and experience the wonderful new you that you truly are!

In your quiet time, let go of your fear about breaking out of your shell, and remember:

*The Power of God is with me, inside my shell,
as well as in the new world outside my shell.
Today, I step out in faith and I dare to be the new me
that has been waiting to come forth!
Thank You, God, for breaking me out of my shell!*

TODAY, I AM GRATEFUL FOR: _____

GOD'S DAY 202 — *Resting in the Presence*

Remember, _____,
(speak your name aloud)

—when your mind drifts into unhappy scenarios or wrestles with a troubling situation, ask this simple question:

"Who's here?"

Let the answer come: *"I am—God is."*

At that instant you will be reminded of the Presence and Power of God—the *I AM* within you, and from that awareness you can turn the problem over to God to solve.

Today, practice staying in the moment and know the *I AM* is with you at every moment, waiting to lift you out of your difficulties.

In your quiet time now, hold this thought:

Lord, thank You for your abiding Presence with me at all times, in every situation.

I know there is nothing to fear for You are always with me. I rest in Your Presence now.

TODAY, I AM GRATEFUL FOR:_____

_____

GOD'S DAY 203 — *Forgiveness*

Remember, _____,
(speak your name aloud)

—you cannot see or touch a resentment,
yet it will weigh heavily on you who carries it.

It is really too heavy a load to carry, for it will rob you of your peace of mind.

Resentment and unforgiveness are contributing psychosomatic factors in the onset of heart trouble, arthritis, and liver problems.

And conversely, forgiving yourself and others is a major healing agent for these health problems.

Today, choose to release all such burdens.

Through the power of forgiveness, free yourself today!

In your quiet time, hold this prayer in your heart as you think of yourself and those that you may be bearing resentment toward.

Through the forgiving love of Jesus Christ
I now forgive myself and others.
I bless and release them to God, in peace.

TODAY, I AM GRATEFUL FOR: _____

_____

GOD'S DAY 204 — *Bread of Life*

Remember, _____,
        (speak your name aloud)

        —the statement by Jesus Christ:

        "I am the Bread of Life..."

What does it mean?

Take it into meditation today.

Breathe in on—*I AM*.

Breathe out on—*the Bread of Life*.

Ask: *What in you is the spiritual bread that nourishes your soul?*

Hear the Christ Presence within saying to you:

> *I AM the Bread of Life.*
> *Take, eat, this is my body.*
> *I AM the Bread of Truth for your mind.*
> *I AM the Bread of Love for your soul.*
> *I AM the Bread of Life for your body.*

Let you prayer be:

> *Lord, thank You for Your Daily Bread of Truth today.*
> *Lord, thank You for Your Daily Bread of Love.*
> *Lord, thank You for Your Daily Bread of Life,*
> *that I may be nourished by Your Holy Presence.*

TODAY, I AM GRATEFUL FOR: _____
_____

GOD'S DAY 205 — *Gratitude*

Remember, _____,
     (speak your name aloud)

     —to put your gratitude to work to lift your spirits!

If you have awakened with an emotional hangover. recognize it as being part of the human mindset of fear and doubt.

Cure yourself with a quick dose of gratitude.

In your mind begin completing these sentences;

I am so grateful for_____

I am so grateful that_____

I am so grateful that I am_____

I am so grateful to be_____

I am so grateful to be free_____

I am so grateful to have_____

I am so grateful to_____

Keep this up for a few minutes, and you will soon feel your gloom lifting and your cheerfulness restored.

TODAY, I AM GRATEFUL FOR: _____

_____

GOD'S DAY 206 — Breathe a Blessing.

Remember, _____,
> (speak your name aloud)

—your breathing is a direct connection with your Source—
the Source of life, love, and infinite wisdom.

When you are feeling anxious, consciously take a deep breath and concentrate on the words *"Peace, Be still."*

Imagine that you are breathing directly into your heart slowly and deliberately. In a few moments your anxiety will dissolve.

If you are concerned about someone, consciously ask yourself:

> *"What is the highest and best thought*
> *that I can breathe for that person?*

Perhaps it may be:

> *God's life is strong within you,*
> *or God's Power goes with you as you travel.*

Breathe in that thought slowly, hold it in mind, and then breathe it out to enfold that person.

The Breath of Life is a sacred gift from God. Use it to breathe out a blessing to yourself and others today.

*TODAY, I AM GRATEFUL FOR:*_____

_____

GOD'S DAY 207 — *Free Will*

Remember, _____,

(speak your name aloud)

—you have free will.

You have the choice to choose the higher path in life or the lower one.

You have the choice to adopt a positive or a negative reaction to events and situations. To meet them with fear, or with faith.

You have the choice to cooperate with your destiny, or fight against it. Your ultimate destiny is conscious union with God and the unfoldment of the radiant beauty of your soul.

You are on a train carrying you through the ages and lifetimes, through many landscapes toward your ultimate destiny. What you chose to do while you are on the train is your affair.

You can chose to sleep through the journey, grumble or complain, help others on the journey, pray, play, decide to carry your baggage or put it down. Each choice will set into motion an effect that will bless you or trouble you. So you might as well make the best of it.

When you come into this life you come in with a certain hand dealt to you. That hand is your past karma. How you play the hand is your choice.

Lord, help me to make the right choices today.

TODAY, I AM GRATEFUL FOR: _____

GOD'S DAY 208 — *Intention*

Remember, _____,
(speak your name aloud)

—to set your intention for today!

Set it, and see it in your mind's eye.

Speak it to yourself—

"Today, I set my intention to _____."

Send your spirit ahead of you to see it accomplished. Your energy, your body will follow along and get it done!

A prison chaplain often used street language to get his point across when teaching self-improvement classes to the prisoners.

He illustrated the point of intention by saying,

"Your behind follows your mind!"

Today, send your right intention ahead of you, and follow along behind!

*TODAY, I AM GRATEFUL FOR:*_____

GOD'S DAY 209 — *Play Day*

Remember, _____,
          (speak your name aloud)

      —to let your inner child out to play today.

Break out of your stodgy adult mindset today. Escape from your straightjacket of conformity and propriety. Give the "god-child" within you an opportunity to speak its wonderful wisdom or break into spontaneous play.

When Jesus was asked by his disciples: "Who is greatest in the kingdom of heaven?" He called a little child to Him and said, *" . . . unless you turn and become like children, you will never enter the kingdom of heaven."* (Matt. 18: 1-3)

Perhaps Jesus was saying to become *child-like*—to have the wonder, the simple trust, the joy and laughter, and the spontaneity of a child!

Go with some friends to a theme park. Ride a roller coaster, get soaked in a wild water ride. Watch the clowns and the mimes and became a child once again!

If you cannot go to a theme park, run barefoot through the grass . . . look with childlike wonder at a spider web glistening with dew like a string of pearls in the morning sun . . . step outside in the rain and let it kiss your face. Give the child in you a warm hug.

Today, experience the wonder and joy of the kingdom right here on Earth! Your little child deserves it!

TODAY, I AM GRATEFUL FOR: _____

_____

GOD'S DAY 210 — *All-Providing Resource*

Remember, _____,
             (speak your name aloud)
                  —*your prosperity is assured.*

Your every need shall be fulfilled as you stay connected to the Source of all Supply.

Your faith is that connection—it opens the flow of abundance to come to you from every direction.

Bank accounts may fail, but God's bank never fails. You can draw upon it in prayer and meditation.

In your quiet time now, meditate on this thought:

I have unbounded faith in God as my all-providing resource.
I see my good flowing to me now from every direction,
and my prosperity is assured.
Thank You, God!

*TODAY, I AM GRATEFUL FOR:*_____

_____

GOD'S DAY 211 — Be Still

Remember, _____,

(speak your name aloud)

—to center down.

When you are feeling tense, scattered, or anxious, take a slow, deep breath, and concentrate on the following verse:

Be still and know that I am God.   (Psalm 46:10)

Now continue with your slow breathing, and let the verse lead you further into God's perfect peace—

Be still and know that I am God

(God —all around you, filling the universe)

Be still and know that I Am

(the Christ within)

Be still and know

(cease thinking, just know)

Be still

(absolute quietness)

Be!

(perfect oneness)

TODAY, I AM GRATEFUL FOR: _____

GOD'S DAY 212 — Blessing

Remember, _____,
   (speak your name aloud)

> *—to bless your way through the day!*

Someone is waiting for your blessing today. Who will it be?

Whisper a silent *Bless You* to this person.

Your blessing opens a connection between God's love, you, and the person you are blessing. You serve as a conduit for God's power to harmonize and heal.

During your daily activities, take a moment to bless everyone and everything around you.

Bless your car—it will work better.

Bless your home, and the people you are working with.

Let your prayer be:

> *Today, I bless my way through the day!*

TODAY, I AM GRATEFUL FOR:_____

_____

GOD'S DAY 213 — *Not by Chance*

Remember, _____,
(speak your name aloud)

*—as waves rise from the ocean, crest, and reach out
to spread forth on the beach—*

—so there are waves of souls eternally rising from the infinite ocean of God's love, flowing in to spread forth on the shores of life.

You have arrived on the shore of this lifetime with many other souls with whom you will interact to learn, to grow, and to serve.

It was not by chance but by Higher Wisdom that you were born into this time in history. Not by chance your place of birth, nor the family your soul chose.

All provided the optimum setting and circumstances for your soul to learn its greatest lessons, and accomplish what it came in to do.

The people in your life are the players in the great drama that includes all of your life. Each of you has a special role to play in each other's lives. Sometimes you play the heavy role, sometimes the comic role, sometimes the hero's role, other times the tragic figure.

Playing off of each other, you can all learn, and achieve your divine potential.

*If you have forgotten your lines, ask the Stage Director—
your Indwelling Christ.*

TODAY, I AM GRATEFUL FOR: _____

_____

GOD'S DAY 214 — Awaken

Remember, _____,
             (speak your name aloud)

    *—you are part of the critical mass now forming
    to lift humanity to its next great awakening.*

You are among the growing numbers of people everywhere sparking the next evolutionary leap to what humanity is destined to be—fully awakened, fully empowered spiritual beings, expressing in full measure the Love, Power, and Wisdom of God that is inherent within them.

Look around you and you will see others of that new enlightened race. You can tell them by the light in their faces and their atmosphere of inner peace.

Let your spiritual understanding and compassion for others lift you to the realization of your true Nature.

Let your prayer be:

Lord, awaken me to the glory of your spirit within me.

*Awaken and empower me to be all that you created me to be.
Help me to express Your love and wisdom to my world today.*

TODAY, I AM GRATEFUL FOR: _____

_____

GOD'S DAY 215 — *Ripple Effect*

Remember, _____,

(speak your name aloud)

—*you are part of the universal ripple effect.*

Have you ever tossed several stones into a pond and watched the ripples spread out?

Each stone creates its own circle of ripples and they spread out to interact with and overlap the ripples of other stones. Yet each maintains its own original pattern.

We are always creating ripples as well as receiving the effects of other people's thoughts and actions. We are all inter-connected in one vast infinite ripple network.

Being true to yourself will enable you to maintain your own pattern in the midst of so many other disturbing patterns.

Be aware of the ripples you are sending out, that they have a beneficial effect on the entire network.

Today I send forth ripples
of God's Love, Light, and Peace!

TODAY, I AM GRATEFUL FOR: _____

_____

GOD'S DAY 216 — *Letter to God*

Remember, _____,
                 (speak your name aloud)

—if you are feeling down today,
write a letter to God about it.

Take a pad and simply begin to tell God all about the trouble that you are disturbed about.

Describe the problem and spill out all the dark emotions you are feeling within yourself. Get them out of your head and heart where they are bottled up, raising your blood pressure, and stressing your heart.

Let the knotted thoughts and feelings unravel themselves at the point of your pen. The more you write, the more your heart will ease.

Next begin to ask questions of God and let the quiet inner Voice answer. It will help if you will write your questions with your dominant hand, and then switch hands and write with your other hand as the answers from the inner Voice come into your mind. Switching hands helps to bypass the conventional mind and opens the way for your intuitive nature to express.

As you converse with God, beautiful insights will flow. The way through your difficulties will be shown.

God is waiting to dialogue with you today!

TODAY, I AM GRATEFUL FOR: _____

GOD'S DAY 217 — *Live in the Kingdom*

Remember, _____,
(speak your name aloud)

—you live in the kingdom and the kingdom lives in you.

The kingdom of heaven, as Jesus taught, is at hand, here, now, within you.

It is the love, the joy, the wisdom, and the power that lives in you at the core of your soul as your spiritual nature, waiting to be touched. Waiting to pour forth through you! Awaken to it today! Get in touch with it!

How, you ask? Why, my goodness—look around you!

It shows itself as beauty, and love, and nature, and the smile on the face of your loved one.

It is the inner strength that comes to you when you are despairing and exhausted.

It is the brilliant flash of an idea that shows you the way out of your unsolvable problem.

Look now for the Kingdom in that Secret Place inside your heart. Take a deep breath and step inside in total adoration and communion. The One Who Loves You with Unconditional Love is waiting there for you.

Let your prayer be:

Beloved Lord, my soul comes into Thy Presence now, heart beating with Joy!

TODAY, I AM GRATEFUL FOR: _____

_____

GOD'S DAY 218 — Sacred Marriage

Remember, _____,
                    (speak your name aloud)

—there is a sacred union within you that cannot be broken.

Your mind and your heart are wedded together for life.

Your thoughts and feelings are continually conceiving and bringing forth multitudes of children that are your future.

If your intellect and your intuition are fighting each other there is no peace in your house.

Your logical, left-brain masculine intellect must learn to love, respect, and give credence to your intuitive, right brain feeling nature. She often knows the way through where your logical sense cannot find a way.

Close your eyes, take a deep breath, and see a sacred marriage being performed in the secret place of the Most High within you.

In your meditation let those two beautiful parts of your nature exchange their vows to love, respect, and believe in each other, in the presence of the high priest, your Indwelling Christ.

*TODAY, I AM GRATEFUL FOR:*_____
_____

GOD'S DAY 219 — *Take the Father's Hand*

Remember, _____,
　　　　　(speak your name aloud)

　　　　　　　—you do not walk alone.

On your journey through life you pass through sunny, carefree days, and days of sadness and gloom—times of joy and times of despair.

If today you are experiencing one of those dark times, remind yourself that you do not walk alone.

The Father walks with you, guiding and protecting you, just as a small boy walks confidently holding on to his beloved father's hand.

In your quiet time now, imagine that loving Presence walking by your side and know that all is well.

Today, remind yourself:

　　　　My hand is in the hand of the Father.
　　　　　　　and all is well.

TODAY, I AM GRATEFUL FOR: _____

_____

GOD'S DAY 220 — Oneness

Remember, _____,
(speak your name aloud)

—you are as God is.

That is the Truth about you.

You are as God is because God is really all there is—the Mind and Essence of all creation, formed and un-formed.

You have no existence apart from God. You draw your intelligence, your spiritual DNA, your life force from that One Source.

Know this for yourself today, and draw upon that Creative Power for every desire and requirement.

Meditate on this Truth now.

I am as God is, and we are one.
I draw on God's Power within me to live,
work, and guide my way through the day.
Thank You, God.

*TODAY, I AM GRATEFUL FOR:*_____

_____

GOD'S DAY 221 — *Dare to be You!*

Remember, _____,
(speak your name aloud)

—you can only be a second-best somebody else.

You are unique in all the world, and the world needs you to be all that you can be.

Have you ever thought or said:

"It's too risky to be myself.
"What if nobody likes who I truly am?
"It's safer to just go along with the crowd and not stand out."

Dare to be you! You can succeed at that, but you'll always fail at being someone else, or being what someone else wants you to be. You don't have to be what your parents want you to be if it is not being true to your own calling. Take the wraps off your creativity. Take the wraps off your potential.

Make a list of your best qualities and know that God gave them to you to use, not hide.

Step out on faith and go for that dream that has been in the back of your mind waiting like a wallflower to be noticed and asked to dance!

Today, I dare to be me!
Today, I dare to express the talents
God has given to me!
Today, I am free to be me!

TODAY, I AM GRATEFUL FOR: _____

_____

GOD'S DAY 222 — *Mirror Talk*

Remember, _____,
> (speak your name aloud)

> *—to stand in front of the mirror today*
> *and look yourself right in the eye.*

Tell yourself the Truth that you are stronger than your fears.

Tell yourself that you are a powerful multi-dimensional being endowed with all the wisdom, strength and creativity that you need to be a success—because you are!

Tell yourself that through the power of the Christ within you have the power to overcome all conditions and all obstacles in your pathway—because you truly do!

Today, tell yourself the Truth, and rejoice!

Let your prayer be:

> *Through the power of the Christ within me,*
> *I have the power to overcome all conditions*
> *and all obstacles in my pathway.*

TODAY, I AM GRATEFUL FOR: _____

_____

GOD'S DAY 223 — New Paradigm

Remember, _____,
            (speak your name aloud)

            —chaos is order in motion.

In the midst of our settled lives, chaos and confusion come to shake us and break us out of our old ruts.

At those times remember the truth that in order for the *new* you to come forth, the *old* you must break up and make way.

Take the higher view that the apparent chaos in your life is the sign that a new and better order is coming forth.

This outer break-up is always frightening to our human self. It fears the cracks in its eggshell—its ego armor. We are like "the egg that was afraid to hatch"—that ended up going rotten inside. Either we dare to hatch out, or we die inside.

Look for the new paradigm that is unfolding. Agree with the process of change.

Hold to the truth that God will bring new good from the ashes of the old, and your spirit will emerge stronger and wiser.

Let your prayer be:

Lord, bring forth the new me from the chaos of my old self.
I am ready to hatch out!!

TODAY, I AM GRATEFUL FOR: _____

_____

GOD'S DAY 224 — Golden Light

Remember, _____,
                (speak your name aloud)

*"He that dwells in the secret place of the most High
shall abide under the shadow of the Almighty."*

Psalm 91

In a moment of contemplation now take refuge in that Secret Place of your heart.

Bask in the Light and Love of God.

Imagine breathing that golden Light into every cell and organ of your being until you are aglow with that Light. Feel your spirits lifting.

Wrap that Light around you as a golden cloak of protection.

Wrap your loved ones safely around with that Light and protection.

Let your prayer be:

*Clothed with God's golden Light
I walk confidently through this day.*

*TODAY, I AM GRATEFUL FOR:*_____

_____

GOD'S DAY 225 — *Agree with Change*

Remember, _____,
　　　　　(speak your name aloud)

　　　　—changes are not adversaries.

Jesus taught us a higher way to handle change.

"Agree with thine adversary (the change that you are resisting) *quickly, while thou art in the way with him; lest at any time the adversary deliver you to the judge, and the judge deliver you to the officer, and thou be cast into prison."*

Find the *point of positive agreement* with the change lest your resistance delivers you to the "judge"—the Law of Cause and Effect—which will "sentence" you to be a "prisoner" of the negative aspects of the change.

The longer you resist, the longer you stay prisoner of the negative aspects of the situation.

Find the *point of agreement* by looking beyond the appearances to the Presence of God waiting to bring forth the good from the situation.

Make that agreement now and open yourself to receive the blessing from the situation.

Let your prayer be:

*I agree with the good in this situation
and I call upon God to bring it forth for me now!
Thank You God!*

TODAY, I AM GRATEFUL FOR: _____

_____

GOD'S DAY 226 — *Open Up and Smile*

. Remember, _____,
(speak your name aloud)

—God is waiting to smile through you today,
so open up and smile!

A friend was out shopping one day and she happened to look into a store window at a display. All of a sudden she saw the face of a rather grim looking girl mirrored back.

To her surprise and consternation, she realized it was she! "My goodness," she said, "is that what I look like?" Immediately she changed her expression for she did not want the world to have to look at that face!

She laughs about it now, and tries to remember to put on a happy face, if not for the world, at least for herself!

Give yourself a smile today! Go to the mirror, look at that person you see and give yourself a big smile and a thumbs up!

Remember, God is waiting to smile through you today, so open up and smile!

In your quiet time now, close your eyes and smile. Picture the faces of your loved ones, and smile. Picture the beauty of the sunrise…and smile!

TODAY, I AM GRATEFUL FOR: _____

GOD'S DAY 227 — *Moving Forward*

Remember, _____,
　　　　　　(speak your name aloud)

　　　　　—life is a series of doors.

Part of your Masters Course in Life is to learn how to open those doors that lead to your good by knocking with faith, prayer, and imagination.

You are also here to learn how to close the door softly on that which is over and done—in gratitude and release.

If the closed door is the death of a loved one, allow yourself time to grieve. But the time will come for you to go forward—for life continually beckons us forward!

If we continue to stand at the closed door, mourning and regretting, we will miss the new doors life is opening on our pathway.

So today, close the door softly behind you and move forward to the new good that awaits you!

Let your prayer be:

　　Today, I close the door softly behind me
　　and move forward to the new good that awaits me!

TODAY, I AM GRATEFUL FOR: _____

_____

GOD'S DAY 228 — *Aglow with Life*

Remember, _____,
>   (speak your name aloud)

> *—as you would breathe on a smoldering ember
> causing it to glow and break into flame—*

—so your prayers breathe life and strength into the lives of those for whom you pray.

If there is someone that you are keeping in your prayers, picture that person now in your meditation.

Imagine taking in a deep breath of God's Light and Love from on High, and then prayerfully breathe out that Light and Love to that person.

See them glowing with the radiant, healing Life of God.

Now, hold that image for yourself.

I am aglow with the radiant, healing Life of God.

*TODAY, I AM GRATEFUL FOR:*_____

_____

GOD'S DAY 229 — *Be Still*

Remember, _____,
     (speak your name aloud)
          —*to let your mind go still.*

Let the TV screen of your mind, with its frenetic images, go blank.

Let the stormy surface of your mind calm down.

In your meditation imagine your mind being a peaceful lake on a summer's day—placid, with hardly a ripple. Watch the sunlight glistening on the silken surface of the water.

To any wandering thoughts speak, *Peace be still.*

Hold this thought:

The peace of God fills my soul, and all is well.

TODAY, I AM GRATEFUL FOR:_____

_____

GOD'S DAY 230 — *Game of Minutes*

Remember, _____,
         (speak your name aloud)

         —*to play the Game of Minutes today.*

See if you can say *Thank You, God,* under your breath for 60 seconds as you walk or drive or work. String together as many minutes as you can.

Try beaming silent blessings to your co-workers on the job for one minute.

Let Nature help you to play the Game.

Take a moment to listen to the birds singing, even the cawing of the crows, and receive their gift of joy. Look into the face of a flower and accept its gift of beauty. Look into the face of a child or a friend, and silently bless them. Let God's love flow from you.

A few minutes into the Game and you will feel joy beginning to flow through you, washing away any gloom that you may have started the day with. You will begin to feel the flow of love moving through you. You will be practicing the Presence of God.

Play the *Game of Minutes* today and let the joy of giving and receiving lift your spirits!

TODAY, I AM GRATEFUL FOR: _____

GOD'S DAY 231 — *Self-Renewal*

Remember, _____,
>   (speak your name aloud)

> —*just as your body needs the Breath of Life*
> *in order to heal and nourish itself,*
> *so your soul needs the Holy Breath of Divine Love*
> *to empower it.*

Rest quietly now and imagine yourself bathed in a ray of divine Light and Love coming down from on High. Feel yourself surrounded and enfolded in that incomparable Love.

Slowly and rhythmically breathe in God's Light and Love. Imagine breathing it in through every pore as a golden stream, and breathing that golden light to each part of your body.

Speak the word:

> *I am a radiating center of Divine Light and Love.*

Meditate on that Love enfusing every organ of your body, every corner of your soul—until you actually feel aglow with that healing Light. Keep this up for ten minutes.

Throughout your day hold the thought:

> *I am a radiating center of Divine Light and Love.*

*TODAY, I AM GRATEFUL FOR:*_____

GOD'S DAY 232 — *Direction*

Remember, _____,
(speak your name aloud)

*—if you don't know where you're going
you'll wind up somewhere else!*

Intention sets your direction and purpose. Take time to do this before beginning any project or task, no matter how simple.

As you set your intention, you direct your inner sight in the direction in which you desire to proceed. Your intention establishes the energy field for fulfillment, so you don't wander aimlessly. Then what comes into your life is not "accidental" but purposeful.

Prior to starting any project, set your intention, and visualize its completion and success.

When you enter your car, set your intention for a safe journey by praying:

The Light of God surrounds and protects me.

Set your intention for success today.

TODAY, I AM GRATEFUL FOR: _____

_____

GOD'S DAY 233 — Healing

Remember, _____,
(speak your name aloud)

—Divine Intelligence knows the perfect DNA
for every cell of your body.

It knows how to recreate and renew your body according to that perfect pattern. That Power is greater than any appearance of illness or disease.

If you have a healing need for yourself or a loved one, hold on to the truth that Divine Intelligence is present in you and your loved one.

Hold this prayer:

The Divine Intelligence that created me
knows how to heal me, and is doing it now!
And I am grateful! Praise God!

*TODAY, I AM GRATEFUL FOR:*_____

GOD'S DAY 234 — *Worry Session*

Remember, _____,
  (speak your name aloud)

—to have a worry session today.

Gather up all those loose worries that pester you like a swarm of gnats and write them down.

Once a week, clear them out by making a list of them.

Today, ask yourself:

What am I worried about?

All sorts of worries will come— from the really big ones— life, death, health, relationships, finances, etc.—to the smallest ones that are really quite silly. But write them down anyhow.

Now, look at them and say:

There is nothing here that God cannot handle.
Right here, right now, I release them to God
to take care of, and I am free.
Thank You, God!

TODAY, I AM GRATEFUL FOR: _____

_____

GOD'S DAY 235 — *End of Your Assignment*

Remember, _____,
            (speak your name aloud)

*—at the right time for your soul's purposes,
you will reach the end of your assignment here on Earth.*

At that appointed time you will have reached the end of your journey of exploration in space/time. It will be time to make the return trip home!

Remember that it is only the body, the Earthly house you live in—that dies. The Real of you, the spiritual nature of you is of God and never ceases to be. It is immortal. It goes on to new assignments under the care and guidance of the Lord of your being.

Remember also that God as Unconditional Love, surrounds and enfolds you as you make the move into the next dimension of Light.

The twenty-third psalm gives this assurance: *"Yea though I walk through the valley of the shadow of death, I shall fear no evil, for thou art with me...."*

So, remember to live one day at a time with confidence, knowing that your soul knows when your time will be to move on.

In the meantime, you are always safe, and God walks with you every step of your way through each day and beyond.

*TODAY, I AM GRATEFUL FOR:*_____

GOD'S DAY 236 — *Length of Your Faith*

Remember, _____,
          (speak your name aloud)

*—you can only walk over the sea of your difficulties
the length of your faith.*

Peter walked on the water for as long as he kept his eyes on his master, Jesus. But as soon as he looked down and saw the stormy sea, he was afraid and sank.

So lift your eyes above the storms of life and fix them steadfastly on the Presence and Power of Christ within, and you will stay on top of your difficulties.

Keep your eyes on the Lord, and you will walk safely the length of your faith today.

Hold this thought today:

*My eyes are ever on the Lord,
and I walk safely over stormy waters to safety.*

TODAY, I AM GRATEFUL FOR: _____

_____

GOD'S DAY 237 — *Ocean of God's Love*

Remember, _____,
       (speak your name aloud)

> *—you live in the ocean of God's Love.*
> *Open up your heart and let God fill it.*

You live in the ocean of God's Truth. Open up your mind and let God fill it with infinite wisdom.

You live in the ocean of God's Life. Open up your pores and let God fill your body with radiant Life.

Let that Life renew and restore you.

As you meditate now, imagine yourself floating serenely in the infinite ocean of God's Love.

Let it support you.

Hold the thought:

> *I live in the ocean of God's Love.*
> *It permeates every atom of my being.*
>
> *I am supported, and provided for*
> *by the infinite ocean of God's abundance.*

TODAY, I AM GRATEFUL FOR: _____

_____

GOD'S DAY 238 — *Emotional Buttons*

Remember, _____,
(speak your name aloud)

—buttons are for pushing!

Let your emotional buttons be pushed. How else will you know what old negative patterns are floating near the surface waiting to be healed?

When someone pushes one of your sore spots, don't get sore about it. Simply observe your reactions.

Stay detached and smile at yourself as you would an angry child—for that is who you were when the button was first created. Every button is connected with an old fear, or an old hurt that needs to be forgiven and healed.

In your meditation now, ask God to lead you back to the unhappy experience where the button was originally created. Ask to be shown the truth about the experience.

Let your prayer be:

Lord, help me to identify and heal this old button.
Lead me back to find that hurtful, frightful time
that needs healing.

Help me to forgive, and to comfort my inner child
so it knows it is safe and loved, and no longer needs to react.
Convert every painful button to a button of love and understand-
ing.

TODAY, I AM GRATEFUL FOR: _____

_____

GOD'S DAY 239 — Band of Angels

Remember, _____,

　　　　(speak your name aloud)

　—to post your angels!

　　　You are always surrounded by an invisible
band of angels whose sole purpose is to look after you. They
need only to be acknowledged and thanked in order to be
better able to care for you.

　　　When you are in a place where you need protection, post
your angels. Mentally image two strong angels walking body-
guard beside you.

　　　Post them around your car in the parking lot.

　　　When you are lost, call upon your angels to lead you to
safety.

　　　When you are concerned about a loved one, post God's
angels around and about them.

　　　Do that now in meditation. See them surrounded and
protected by bright angels.

　　*Remember, " . . . he shall give his angels charge over You,
to keep You in all thy ways." Psalm. 91:11*

*TODAY, I AM GRATEFUL FOR:*_____

GOD'S DAY 240 — *God's Beloved*

Remember, _____,
(speak your name aloud)

—*you are God's beloved!*

Speak this to yourself when that accusing voice within you begins to criticize you and put you down—saying that you are not good enough, not worthy enough, not smart enough, not beautiful enough.

These are all lies told by the father of lies—the frightened, little insecure personal self of you that has forgotten its spiritual origin. It never feels safe, never feels loved, never feels equal to life's challenges. It desperately needs to be in control to feel safe.

Remember the Truth about yourself—that you are a beloved child of God—infinitely loved and worthy.

You have a purpose for being in the world—to be a unique expression of the love, wisdom and creativity of your Creator.

Today, meditate on these ideas:

I am God's beloved!
I am unique and valuable to God's purposes.
I have a part to play in the great scheme of the universe.

I am being shown that part now, and I am being given
all the wisdom, strength, and resources necessary
to carry out that role one day at a time.

TODAY, I AM GRATEFUL FOR: _____

GOD'S DAY 241 — *Soul Remodeling*

Remember, _____,

        (speak your name aloud)

—if your life and affairs seem to be in chaos right now, it is a sign that you are undergoing a major "soul remodeling."

Just as when you remodel a house it creates temporary chaos to make way for new beauty, so remodeling your house of consciousness also creates temporary chaos in your outer affairs.

Old walls of limitation and lies are torn down, and new skylights are installed to bring God's Light and Wisdom into your soul.

Take courage and be patient with yourself, for your new "house" will be beautiful. All is proceeding according to the plan of the Master Architect and Builder.

In your quiet time now, thank Christ, the Master Builder, for laying a new foundation in you. Know that out of this chaos will come a new and more splendid you!

Remind yourself:

With courage and patience, I create a new life for myself according to the plan of Christ, the Master Builder.

TODAY, I AM GRATEFUL FOR: _____

GOD'S DAY 242 — *Right Expression*

Remember, _____,
            (speak your name aloud)

*—it is always later than you think, but you have all the time
you need to accomplish that which you came to accomplish!*

You have been growing spiritually and your values have
been changing. In your new spiritual awareness you may find
yourself yearning for work that makes more of a difference in
the world—that contributes to the well being of people and of
our mother planet.

Ask yourself this question:

*If I could be anything I wanted to be in life, and had the
energy, time and resources to be it, what would I really love to be?*

I would really love to be _____

I would really love to be _____

I would really love to be _____

You may have just written the seed ideas for a new
career. Explore the possibilities of it. Follow any leads that
intersect your pathway. Be willing to follow your Inner Guidance.

Remember:

*Working with God, all things are possible—
for with God it is never too late!*

TODAY, I AM GRATEFUL FOR: _____

_____

GOD'S DAY 243 — *Imaging Power*

Remember, _____,
   (speak your name aloud)

—your imagination is your grappling hook that you throw forward to hook onto your dream and pull yourself toward.

What is it you deeply desire? Hook on to it.

Hold that image firmly in mind and persistently view it as already gained.

Make it a virtual reality experience. Feel what it would be like to have already achieved it. Rejoice in it and give thanks for it now, before it has actually shown forth in physical form. What is accomplished in spirit is already on its way.

Totally surrender your desire to the Higher Will. Let go and let the Higher Will bring it about according to that Higher Wisdom.

Let your prayer be:

Loving Lord of my life, here is my desire.
Do with it as You will.
I totally trust that Your Will for me is Absolute Good.
Let Your loving Will be done.

TODAY, I AM GRATEFUL FOR: _____

GOD'S DAY 244 — *Eyes of Faith*

Remember, _____,
(speak your name aloud)

—to see your way clearly today.

See clearly with eyes of faith that God always has given you, is now giving you, and always will give you your 'daily bread'—the good that you desire and require.

Let the clouds of doubt and fear, and the blurriness of disbelief now be dissolved, as you focus on God's goodness.

Let your prayer be:

I see my way clearly with eyes of faith.
I see my way confidently with eyes of faith.
I see my good coming into my life right now,
and I am grateful!
Praise God!

TODAY, I AM GRATEFUL FOR: _____

_____

GOD'S DAY 245 — *Let Your Light Shine*

Remember, _____,
(speak your name aloud)

—we are the Energy of God in denser form.

Clairvoyants can see our bodies as they actually are—radiant energy forms glowing with Light and Love.

Light is at the center of every atom of the body temple.

We are, as Jesus told us, truly the "light of the world."

We are here to let our light shine, and the only way we can do that is through Love—by being radiating centers of God's love.

Today in your meditation, image yourself as a being of Light.

Think of someone for whom you have been praying. Send forth from your heart a beam of God's Light and Love to bless them. See them surrounded and enfolded in that Light and Love.

Let your Light shine!

TODAY, I AM GRATEFUL FOR: _____

GOD'S DAY 246 — *Prayer Power*

Remember, _____,
        (speak your name aloud)

—be not dismayed by the difficulties in your life.
You have immediately available to you the greatest power
on Earth—prayer power.

Like electricity, no one knows exactly what prayer is, but that it works, is indisputable.

Through effective prayer you access the full power of God.

Here are three steps in praying:

First, give thanks that God is at work in your situation right now.

Secondly, know that no person, condition, or appearance has any power over you for God is in charge.

Finally, give your concern to God in total trust and surrender, knowing that all will be done according to that Higher Will for the highest good of all concerned. "Thy Will Be done."

In your quiet time now, follow these three steps as you give your concerns to God.

Give thanks.
Surrender.
Let God's Good will be done.

TODAY, I AM GRATEFUL FOR: _____

The Only Power

*The Real Self of you
is the Only Real Power in your life.*

*It is the Presence of the Infinite in you.
It is always with you—Omnipresence.*

*It is All-Powerful—it creates, it maintains,
And it destroys—Omnipotence.
It is All-Wise and All-Knowing—*

*It gives you all the answers and guidance
you will ever need—Omniscience.*

*It is the Love of you.
It is the Life of you.
It is the Real of you—eternal.*

*Give it all honor and praise.
Love it and make it central.
Make it the Center of your visioning, your thinking,
speaking, feeling and acting.*

There is none else.

*"Look unto me, and be ye saved . . .
for I am God,
and there is none else."
—Isaiah 45: 22*

GOD'S DAY 247 — *The Gift of Time*

Remember, _____,
(speak your name aloud)

*—you start each day with a bank account of 86,000 seconds.
Spend it wisely.*

Every night the bank cancels out whatever time you have failed to invest to a good purpose.

Each day it opens a new account with you. Each night it burns the records of the day. If you fail to use the day's deposits, the loss is yours. There is no going back. There is no drawing against "Tomorrow."

It is up to you to invest this precious fund of hours, minutes, and seconds in order to get the highest rate of return in health, happiness, and success!

Today look upon time as a gift. Invest it in doing things that you believe are important and worthwhile.

When you go to bed at night you will feel an inner satisfaction that you have not only *spent* but *invested* your time well!

*God is blessing you with a new day.
Invest it wisely and well!*

TODAY, I AM GRATEFUL FOR: _____

_____

GOD'S DAY 248 — *Transformation*

Remember, _____,
            (speak your name aloud)

—God's love is the greatest transforming power on Earth.

Use it today to transform your weaknesses into strengths.

In your meditation time, let your prayer be:

*Through the Power of God's Love
I love my weaknesses into strengths,
    —my faults into virtues,
—my laziness into follow-through,
    —my lack into abundance,
        —my lust into pure love.*

*I love my limitations into freedom,
    —my hurts into wholeness,
—my selfishness into service.*

*I am ready to sacrifice the worthless
for the worthwhile—the Holy Worth.*

*Lord, transform me at soul depth
into what you want me to be.*

Amen.

TODAY, I AM GRATEFUL FOR: _____
_____

GOD'S DAY 249 — *Intersection with Destiny*

Remember, _____,
(speak your name aloud)

*—right where you are on your path in life
is exactly where you are supposed to be.*

Everything you have done up to now has prepared you for the right work that is yours to do. You are about to intersect with your destiny.

You would not have been ready before now because you had neither the higher understanding nor the willingness.

All of your so-called mistakes and regrets about what you should have done and didn't (or did do and shouldn't have) were part of your training to prepare you for this new opportunity to make a difference in the world.

As you pray about it, God will reveal to you what you need to know, and will guide and provide for you along your way.

*Lord, I am ready to intersect with my destiny.
Reveal to me what it is that you have prepared me
to do and be.*

*With faith and an open heart,
I listen to your inner Voice.*

TODAY, I AM GRATEFUL FOR: _____

_____

GOD'S DAY 250 — God's Secret Agent

Remember, _____,

       (speak your name aloud)

       —you are God's secret agent.

That is your true assignment here. That is what you came into this world to be.

Secret, in that you are to do your work of sharing God's Light, Love, and Abundance anonymously if at all possible.

Agent, in that you are here to act in behalf of the One who sent you—to help, to lift, to encourage, and provide as needed.

Most of your work can be done silently, in the way of giving a silent blessing to someone—at work, or at home, or on the street.

No one has to know what you are doing. Just go about your daily business. But your silent blessing is bringing God's Light into confused minds. You are bringing God's Love into the hearts of those who are arguing. You are bringing order where there is chaos and dysfunction.

Today, remember to do your blessing work.

God's work depends on it.

*TODAY, I AM GRATEFUL FOR:*_____

_____

GOD'S DAY 251 — *Rise Above Problems*

Remember, _____,
                  (speak your name aloud)

*—struggle as you might, you'll not find an answer to your
problem on the level of the problem.*

The problem has no power to solve itself. Come up higher.
Lift up your mind to the Higher Wisdom, where all answers
reside.

Psalm 121 begins:

*I will lift up mine eyes unto the hills
From whence cometh my help.
My help cometh from the Lord,
who made heaven and Earth...*

Meditate on these truths now.

In your meditation now, imagine yourself climbing up a
hill to a small white chapel on the rise. Enter in the quiet
interior.

Rest there for awhile. The Master comes to sit by you.
Talk over your problem with him. When you feel peace in
your heart you will know what you need to know, and what
you need to do.

Your help comes from the Lord. Be grateful.

TODAY, I AM GRATEFUL FOR: _____

_____

GOD'S DAY 252 — *Mind of Christ*

Remember, _____,
   (speak your name aloud)

> *—when you have a test to take,*
> *remember the Mind of Christ in you.*

Relying on your own memory can fail, but the Mind of Christ within you can never fail.

Whether it is a test you need to take, a speech you need to make, or important facts you need to recall—call upon the all-knowing Mind of Christ for help.

At the time of your need, let your prayer be:

> *I am one with the all-knowing Mind of Christ.*
> *I know, I remember, and I understand.*
>
> *The right words come to me in perfect sequence*
> *and I express myself perfectly.*
> *Thank You, Lord.*

TODAY, I AM GRATEFUL FOR: _____

_____

GOD'S DAY 253 — *Higher Purpose*

Remember, _____,
(speak your name aloud)

*—you are here to become consciously aware
of what you already are at the very core of your being.*

Your personality and body are the costumes you wear during this awakening and empowering process. And just as a child outgrows last year's clothes, so you change your costumes as you grow.

Your personal will must serve this Higher Purpose, ("Not my will, but Thy Will be done")—and in the process it becomes refined and spiritualized.

Your body is transforming as well as it feels the Higher Energies coursing through it, renewing and raising its vibrations to a higher level of health.

Today, offer your will, your mind, and your body to this Higher Purpose.

Let your prayer be:

*Here I am, Lord,
help me to grow into what you desire me to be.*

TODAY, I AM GRATEFUL FOR: _____

GOD'S DAY 254 — Praise

Remember, _____,
(speak your name aloud)

—where there is no love all faults are magnified.

This is especially true of children and teenagers.

Focus on their best qualities, their best actions, not the worst. Whatever you love and praise in them will magnify and become dominant in their nature.

Likewise giving your energy to their worst characteristics only magnifies them.

Switch to loving the goodness of God that is inherent within them. Love the Presence of God in them.

Let your prayer for them be:

*I praise the goodness of God
growing stronger in you everyday!*

*TODAY, I AM GRATEFUL FOR:*_____

_____

GOD'S DAY 255 — *Strength*

Remember, _____,
         (speak your name aloud)

       —when you feel like giving up, keep on keeping on.

Do you wonder if you will ever succeed in a certain endeavor or in the fulfillment of your heart's desire?

Keep on knowing that with God as your partner, all things will work together for good.

Keep on doing what is yours to do, knowing that God is doing the rest.

Keep on praying in the midst of doubt.

Keep on trusting even though your heart grows faint with fear.

Do not give in to despair, but *keep on keeping on!* —and you will fulfill the desires of your heart!

Hold this thought:

      I can do all things through Christ
        that strengthens me.

TODAY, I AM GRATEFUL FOR: _____

_____

GOD'S DAY 256 — *Perspective*

Remember, _____,
> (speak your name aloud)

> *—you look at your world through the lenses*
> *of your prejudices, mind-set and feelings.*

What color mental and emotional eyeglasses are you wearing? Are they colored with fear and anger, or beauty and compassion?

How do you see yourself? With dark glasses of limitation and self-doubt, or with the higher vision to see through to the true and the beautiful that lies latent within you?

In the difficult situation facing you, can you see God at work behind the scenes to bring forth new good?

In the troubled teenager, can you see the splendid soul struggling to emerge out of its cocoon of self-doubt and awkwardness?

If you don't like what you see, you can change your attitudes—your inner lenses. Switch from taking a negative view of yourself and others to seeing the Good.

Hold this thought for yourself:

> *I see with eyes of love, and harmony prevails!*

TODAY, I AM GRATEFUL FOR:_____

GOD'S DAY 257 — *Safe Place*

Remember, _____,
                    (speak your name aloud)

—to ask yourself:

> " *Is everyone safe in my house of consciousness?*
> *Is everyone safe to walk down*
> *the streets of my mind?"*

If you are harboring any resentment or anger toward someone, it is not safe for them to be in your "house" or on your "street."

If in your mind's eye you are picturing yourself harming another or angrily "giving them a piece of your mind," make peace now, for those thoughts and emotions reflect back to hurt you and affect your own health as well as theirs. We are all connected at the soul level, and what hurts one hurts all.

Give up those old mental scenarios for positive ones. Let go and fully forgive.

In your quiet time now, visualize Jesus Christ being with you and the other person. See Christ acting as a mediator, establishing peace between the two of you.

Let your prayer be:

> *Lord, make peace between us.*
> *Help me to understand that their pain and hurt*
> *is a mirror of my own.*
> *Let your forgiving love wipe out all misunderstandings*
> *and give us peace.*

TODAY, I AM GRATEFUL FOR: _____

_____

GOD'S DAY 258 — *You are not a Victim*

Remember, _____,
(speak your name aloud)

—you are not a victim unless you make yourself to be.

You can only be a victim of your own negative reactions to life's experiences. In that respect you create your life and experiences.

You make things happen. You create calamity and you create success. You create misery and you create joy. You make yourself sick and you make yourself well.

Take charge of your thinking and visioning. Get your mind out of the gutter of fear and doubt.

Thoughts of love, thoughts of praise and high visioning will lift you out of the pit of frustration and despair.

Start thinking those thoughts now. Turn within to that Universal Higher Power from which you draw your power to think and feel and act. Hold the following thoughts in meditation now.

From the place of God's Love in my heart,
I love my world, I love the people in my world,
I love my work.

I praise the goodness of God at work in my life.
I praise the goodness of God at work in the people in my life.

I am sustained and supported by the goodness of God.
and I am grateful!

TODAY, I AM GRATEFUL FOR: _____
_____

GOD'S DAY 259 — *Encouragement*

Remember, _____,
(speak your name aloud)

*—it is better to light one candle,
than to curse the darkness.*

Each day it is good to ask yourself,

*"Am I making the corner of my world
brighter?
Am I lighting candles,
or just complaining about what's wrong?"*

Will you speak a sincere word of encouragement to a person who is feeling low today? Will you call or write to someone who is alone and perhaps feeling forgotten?

Will you take time to whisper a prayer or blessing for someone in need of strength?

If you do any or all of these things, you will be bringing light to your corner of the world —and you will be blessed in return!

TODAY, I AM GRATEFUL FOR: _____

GOD'S DAY 260 — Resurrection and Life

Remember, _____,
              (speak your name aloud)

              —this statement by Jesus Christ:

I am the resurrection and the life.

What does it mean?

Meditate upon it, and then during the day, use it as a mantra to repeat to yourself over and over. Put the words on a little card for your pocket or desk.

Let the statement break itself open in your mind and reveal the true meaning of I AM in you.

In your meditation now, as you hear the words silently, ask:

Who in you is speaking these words?

What is being resurrected in you?

What in you is dead and is being brought to life?

By whom?

Let the words *I am the resurrection and the life* feed and renew you—spiritually, mentally, emotionally, financially and physically, today.

*TODAY, I AM GRATEFUL FOR:*_____

_____

GOD'S DAY 261 — *Spiritual Birthright*

Remember, _____,
　　　　　(speak your name aloud)

　　　　　　—your divine potential.

What would happen if you took Jesus at his word when he said *"Ye are gods..."?* (John 10:34)

He was speaking about our higher nature—the spirit of God, the divine spark at the core of our immortal soul.

What would happen if you dared to accept that truth about yourself, and began to think, act, and live your life from that marvelous Presence within you?

What would happen if you actually accepted your spiritual potential and began to live from it?

Imagine the love, joy, wisdom, and power you would feel! Imagine being set free of your fears, anxieties, and self-defeating beliefs.

Today, dare to think, speak, and work from this Higher Self—your god-self, which Jesus called the Father within.

To help you remember, speak the following statement to yourself as you go about your daily tasks.

See how it changes your view of yourself, lifts your spirits, and empowers you.

　　Not I, but the Father with me is doing this work.

TODAY, I AM GRATEFUL FOR: _____

GOD'S DAY 262 — *Yesterdays*

Remember, _____,
        (speak your name aloud)

     —to give your yesterdays to God.

Let them go so you can live fully and freely in the Now Moment. Why let your unhappy memories chain you like a slave to the past.

God has new blessings waiting for you right now, but you cannot see them if your mind is dwelling in yesterday. No matter how bad your past may have been, it's over. Like last week's newspapers, it's only good for re-cycling.

The best way to re-cycle the past is to give your yesterdays to God.

In your quiet time now, hold this prayer:

Loving Lord, here is my past, I give it to you.
Take my yesterdays and transform them with your love.
I am now open and receptive to the blessings
you have for me today!

*TODAY, I AM GRATEFUL FOR:*_____

_____

GOD'S DAY 263 — *The Lion Within You.*

Remember, _____,
  (speak your name aloud)

  —the picture of a house cat sitting in front of a large mirror looking at a magnificent lion staring back at him!

  You have a mighty lion inside of you!"

  We have hundreds of self-image portraits in our subconscious art gallery. The way we are acting at any given time reflects which self-image we've identified with and is ruling our life.

  There are all kinds of pictures in that gallery—childhood pictures, loser pictures, victim pictures, as well as confident and successful ones.

  There is also, in a beautiful upper room of the art gallery all by itself, a stunning portrait of who you really are—a radiant, powerful, serenely confident, peace-filled spiritual being—free, wise and immortal. The image of God in you.

  Rarely do you visit that upper room, because you don't feel worthy of that image. So you usually wander around on the lower floors of the gallery and only identify with the limited images.

  Today, in your meditation, visit that upper room and look long at that image, and say to yourself. *"I am that!"*

TODAY, I AM GRATEFUL FOR: _____

_____

GOD'S DAY 264 — *Solar Eclipse*

Remember, _____,
(speak your name aloud)

*—the sun still shines during the darkness
of a solar eclipse.*

Imagine how frightening an eclipse must have been to ancient peoples. What dark power was killing the Sun God?

When troubles overshadow our faith in God, we often wonder whether we will ever be happy again.

One moment our life is bright and we are healthy and happy. Then a small shadow of trouble slides almost unnoticed into our life. Soon the darkness grows stronger and totally eclipses our happiness.

We carry on in dread and gloom—losing faith, falling into despair. But there shines a corona of light radiating from behind the trouble. Keep your eye on that circle of hope.

Hold firm to the truth that the Son-Light of God still shines behind the darkness of trouble. Watch as the shadow begins to slide away. Every moment the Light and Power of God is emerging triumphant.

Let your prayer be:

*I hold fast in faith to the truth that no darkness
can overcome the Light and Power of God in my life.
I have nothing to fear. All troubles are passing.
God's light shines triumphant.*

*TODAY, I AM GRATEFUL FOR:*_____
_____

GOD'S DAY 265 — Green Light

Remember, _____,,
         (speak your name aloud)

        —to give faith the green light!

Stop your worrying! You've got the green light!

Open up the traffic jam of worry thoughts in your mind and let faith through!

Stop worrying about yourself, your age, and your circumstances.

Stop worrying about your health, your finances, and your relationships.

Give faith the green light!

Give God the go-ahead signal to take charge of your life and move you forward!

You've got the green light!

Go!

Let your prayer be:

        I move forward with faith!
        I've got the green light today!

TODAY, I AM GRATEFUL FOR: _____

_____

GOD'S DAY 266 — Trust in the Mystery

Remember, _____,,
          (speak your name aloud)

        —to trust in the Great Mystery.

Beyond the Law of Mind that states we make our own world through the action of our thoughts, visualizations, and feeling—there is a great Mystery that introduces the Unexpected in our life.

You tread a slippery slope in life.

Just when you think you've got it all figured out, nice, safe, and secure, the Great Mystery kicks in and your feet slip out from under you.

Slipping and sliding downhill, fearing the worst, you careen right into another world of wonder, joy, and unexpected blessings!

Relax from your worries about security and learn to trust in the Great Mystery that God loves you and loves to surprise you with unexpected goodies!

       Take a sled ride with God today!

*TODAY, I AM GRATEFUL FOR:*_____

_____

GOD'S DAY 267 — *Focus*

Remember, _____,
(speak your name aloud)

—to focus on your goal today.

Just as a ship drifts at sea when there is no clear destination, so our thoughts, without a focused goal, drift aimlessly into trouble.

What is the good you seek? How would you like your life to be?

In your meditation today, focus your thought energy on the good you desire, and release all mental images of doubt or fear.

The universe is a giving universe, and is waiting for you to concentrate on your desire so it can bring it forth for you.

Today, as you focus on the good you desire, you will hasten the bringing forth of that good into your life!

TODAY, I AM GRATEFUL FOR: _____

GOD'S DAY 268 — *Power of Praise*

Remember, _____,
(speak your name aloud)

*—the power of praise is the power
to bring good into your life.*

Today when you feel an urge to criticize or complain, stop and take a moment to see what is right and good in the situation.

Praise that good and watch it increase, for praise is the power of increase.

Concentrate on the good in your life now, as you speak these words to yourself:

I praise and give thanks for the Spirit of God within me.

*I praise and give thanks for my good body.
It is a temple of God, and a faithful friend to me.*

*I praise and give thanks for my home.
No matter how humble it may be, it provides shelter and
privacy for me.*

*I praise and give thanks for my work.
It is an opportunity to express my God-given qualities
and abilities.*

*I praise and give thanks for all the beauty around me,
and I see more and more beauty every day.
I praise and give thanks for the people in my life.
We are together by divine appointment.*

*TODAY, I AM GRATEFUL FOR:*_____

_____

GOD'S DAY 269 — *Choose Peace*

Remember, _____,
         (speak your name aloud)

—your emotions drive your actions.

At frequent intervals during the day, stop and ask:

"What am I feeling right now?"

As you stand back and observe yourself getting angry and defensive, or feeling sorry for yourself, choose peace instead of the negativity.

A good reminder is to say to yourself:

"I could choose peace instead of this."

Whatever the negative thoughts and feelings are, give them over to your Higher Power to dissolve.

Simply say,

"Take it, Higher Power."

TODAY, I AM GRATEFUL FOR: _____

_____

GOD'S DAY 270 — God Calling

Remember, _____,
(speak your name aloud)

—*God is always calling you, but your line is usually busy.*

Take time right now to check your "call waiting."

God's messages come to you most clearly when you are quiet inside, and even when you are not, God wedges them in between your hurried thoughts.

Be alert to those synchronous so-called coincidences that come your way.

Be alert to a word or phrase that lights up during a conversation with a friend.

Be alert to the lyrics of a song playing in the background.

God's messages are everywhere.

Be alert today.

God is trying to get your attention to tell you how much you are loved

*TODAY, I AM GRATEFUL FOR:*_____

_____

GOD'S DAY 271 — *Nature Break*

Remember, _____,
(speak your name aloud)

—to take a nature break today.

John Burroughs, the great naturalist, wrote:
"it is so easy to get lost in the world."

Nature is our first home and we feel lost in the concrete jungles and artificial life styles we have created for ourselves.

Our soul yearns for the ancient nourishment of the green Earth. Our eyes, cramped by nearsighted computer and television screens—need to gaze upon the limitless horizons of the azure sea and sky.

Today get reconnected with your ancient roots.

Take yourself to a park, and breathe in the fresh smell of the flowers and greenery. Breathe out stress and anxiety.

Slow the pace of your restless mind to the tranquil peace of the trees, their leaves lazy in the gentle breeze.

Watch the wild creatures and learn from them.

Let your mind unwind its tangle of thoughts. Let the ancient tranquility of Nature seep into your soul and restore your peace. Take a nature break today.

*TODAY, I AM GRATEFUL FOR:*_____

GOD'S DAY 272 — *Super-Abundance*

Remember, _____,
      (speak your name aloud)

—your every need shall be fulfilled when you connect
in mind with the Source of All Abundance.

Your faith and imagination makes that connection. The
Source will provide for you to the degree of your trust, and
according to your power to imagine your desire as being
already provided, already yours.

Put your faith, trust and imagination to work for you
today.

Declare:

I have unbounded faith in God as my All-providing Supply.
In faith I believe, in faith I conceive.

It is being done unto me now according to my faith,
and according to my thanksgiving.

Thank You, God!

TODAY, I AM GRATEFUL FOR: _____

_____

GOD'S DAY 273 — *Loved Ones*

Remember, _____,
          (speak your name aloud)

*—to trust the Spirit of God within your loved ones
to lead them in the way of their highest good.*

When someone you love is going down what you judge to be the wrong path, it is only natural to want to help.

Take whatever positive steps you can, but do not try to control them. They will only resist. They have to find their own way.

Remember, their soul has come into this classroom called life with a course of lessons that will lead them to self-mastery. And that often includes going through some very difficult learning experiences.

If you look back on your own life you will see that the life lessons you found so hard to take were the only way by which you could find yourself.

You can best help your loved ones by trusting in their Higher Self—the Spirit of God in them—to lead them safely through the experiences they need for their soul's growth.

In your quiet time think of them now and see them surrounded by God's Light and Love as a protective shield around them. Pray:

*I trust the Presence of God in you
to lead you safely through to your highest good.*

*TODAY, I AM GRATEFUL FOR:*_____

_____

GOD'S DAY 274 — *Mental Ruts*

Remember, _____,

        (speak your name aloud)

     —your thoughts can give you a headache.

They are the ones that hold you in the ruts and patterns that limit you and create trouble for you.

If you are going to change your life for the better, first change your consciousness. There is no other way to lift yourself out of your ruts and self-defeating thought patterns. There is no other way to cure your headache.

Today, take the following new thoughts into your meditation. Let them lift you out of your old mental ruts, and help you to see yourself in a new way.

Post them on your mirror, and carry them in your pocket for thirty days, and speak them aloud to yourself.

     Today I see myself as I truly am—
         beloved and worthy.

     Today I see myself as I truly am—
         unique and capable.

TODAY, I AM GRATEFUL FOR: _____

GOD'S DAY 275 — *Make a Difference*

Remember, _____,
>   (speak your name aloud)

>   *—to make a difference today.*

A wise grandmother advised her grandchildren:

> *"Wherever your lives may lead,*
> *make the world a bit better and more beautiful*
> *because you have lived in it."*

Ask yourself, today:

In what ways can I make my world a bit better and more beautiful—at home, at work, in the neighborhood, and in the society I live in?

The smallest of blessings can make a difference, the smallest of actions can tip the dominoes of life—starting a chain reaction of goodness.

Today, let your prayer be:

> *Here I am, Lord, use me to make a*
> *difference in the world.*

*TODAY, I AM GRATEFUL FOR:*_____

GOD'S DAY 276 — *Living Bridge*

Remember, _____,
        (speak your name aloud)

        —you are a living bridge.

You have the privilege, as well as the responsibility, to bridge the Truth you know to those still living in the ignorance of their fear-based material consciousness.

Yours it is to love them with the unconditional love that sees the divine in them and bring it forth.

Yours it is to deliver them from their fear of death by gently reminding them they are eternal beings.

Yours it is to love them until they awaken to the Presence of God in themselves, and begin to live a life of trusting in that Presence.

You are the bridge. Extend your hand and help them across.

In your meditation time, see yourself being God's bridge, reaching out to help others across..

TODAY, I AM GRATEFUL FOR: _____

_____

GOD'S DAY 277 — A New Day

Remember, _____,
(speak your name aloud)

> *—today is a priceless gift.*
> *Invest it wisely.*

Will you invest today in lasting pursuits —such as mental and spiritual study, service, appreciation, exercise and renewal—or will you let it slip away in useless activities, only to feel remorseful at day's end?

A gift of a new day awaits you. Consider how you will invest it.

Go forth with gratitude as your day unfolds in beauty and joy!

Let your prayer be:

Lord, thank You for a brand new day of opportunity!

TODAY, I AM GRATEFUL FOR: _____

GOD'S DAY 278 — *Open Door*

Remember, _____,
(speak your name aloud)

—the statement by Jesus Christ:
"I am the door."

In your meditation today contemplate the meaning.

Converse with the Presence within you that is speaking the words.

What is the door? Where does it lead?

The Indwelling Christ is the "door" through which you enter into the Secret Place of the Most High.

Picture that door at the center of your spiritual heart.

Think of the verses in the Bible:

"Knock and it shall be opened unto you..."

"Behold, I stand at the door and knock..."

"I have set before thee an open door

which no man can shut..."

Enter with humble praise and thanksgiving.

TODAY, I AM GRATEFUL FOR: _____

_____

GOD'S DAY 279 — *Imaging the Highest*

Remember, _____,

(speak your name aloud)

—you are made in God's image and likeness.

That is, you are endowed with the *image-making* power of God. You are endowed with that supreme creative power called imagination.

That divine power is active within you every moment of the day. Asleep in your dreams or awake, that power is endlessly imaging and creating.

It is your responsibility to direct its activities for your highest good.

How are you using that divine power today—constructively or destructively?

In your meditation now, image the highest and best for yourself—your health, your relationships, your career.

*TODAY, I AM GRATEFUL FOR:*_____

_____

GOD'S DAY 280 — *Your Body is Your Child*

Remember, _____,
        (speak your name aloud)

      —your body is always listening.
      Be careful what you say to it!

Your body is your child, your creation.

What are you feeding it? What are you teaching it?

Are you letting it run and play and build up its muscles and stamina?

Are you treating it with love and respect, or are you abusing it?

Are you raising it to be a lazy child, or are you gently training it to be all that it can be?

You are its father and mother, its teacher, its coach. It depends on you.

Give your child the gift of your love and attention today.

TODAY, I AM GRATEFUL FOR: _____

_____

GOD'S DAY 281 — Recovery

Remember, _____,
             (speak your name aloud)

*   —there is Something that loves you*
*   with everlasting love.*

Something that loves you no matter how badly you make a mess of your life. It is always there with every beat of your heart.

To this Infinite Love you can gladly surrender because you can trust It. Without that Love there is no motive to recover and heal.

Without that Love there is no use trying to put the broken pieces of your life back together again. All recovery efforts fail.

The pieces cannot be put back together in their old flawed pattern. They can only be reassembled in a new way by your Higher Self in a new pattern and glued together by Divine Love.

Today, remember there is Something within you that loves you with everlasting love.

Let your prayer be:

Loving Lord, rebuild me in Thy image.

TODAY, I AM GRATEFUL FOR: _____

_____

GOD'S DAY 282 — *Pocket Prayers*

Remember, _____,
         (speak your name aloud)

    —to carry some pocket prayer power today.

Write out a brief prayer on a small card, date it, laminate it, and carry it in your pocket where you will see it during the day.

It may be a healing prayer, or one for harmony in relationships, or career success or prosperity

Every time you reach into your pocket for your keys or money, you will be reminded of that positive prayer.

After a time the prayer will be completely memorized and become a part of your permanent consciousness.

Here is one that you may choose to use:

    With a new heart and a new spirit,
    I begin anew today!

TODAY, I AM GRATEFUL FOR: _____

_____

GOD'S DAY 283 — *Transmitter*

Remember, _____,
(speak your name aloud)

—to be a transmitter of God's Light and Love today.

The world desperately needs your prayers to bring peace to places of strife and violence, and light and love to people without hope.

Begin first with your own inner world in need of healing. In your meditation, speak silently to yourself:

I breathe in God's Peace,
I breathe out stress and anxiety.

I breathe in God's Love,
I breathe out fear and doubt.

I breathe in God's Light,
I breathe out discouragement and despair.

Now, think of the people and places on Earth in need of blessing. Imagine a great shaft of God's Light coming down and shining into your heart. Let your heart, like a prism, reflect that Light out to shine on the persons or situations that come to mind. Silently speak:

God's Light, Go forth!
God's Love, Go forth!

Send it forth as you breathe out to the persons and places you have chosen. Today, be a transmitter of God's light and love.

*TODAY, I AM GRATEFUL FOR:*_____

GOD'S DAY 284 — *Freedom*

Remember, _____,
　　　　　(speak your name aloud)

> *—to avoid those two taskmasters—*
> *"should have" and "have to."*

The first burdens you with guilt from the past, and the second pressures you with anxiety about the future.

Escape their tyranny by calling yourself back to the present moment.

Hold this thought:

> *I let go of past mistakes and future worries.*
> *Right here, right now, this very moment*
> *God is with me helping me to accomplish all*
> *that needs to be accomplished today.*

TODAY, I AM GRATEFUL FOR: _____

_____

GOD'S DAY 285 — *Perfect Union*

Remember, _____,
                    (speak your name aloud)

                    —you are two in nature.

The ancient bond of yang and yin, the Yah and the Weh, the modern animus and the anima, the head and the heart, the logical and the intuitive, the left and the right, the strong and the tender, the creator and the nurturer.

Let there be a holy bond between them. Let the two be in balance as equals.

Under the Infinite grace and blessing of the Christ, the High Priest within you, let there be a Holy Marriage.

Let the two become one in you, yet each fully present in perfect harmony.

In your meditation hold this thought:

Lord, by Your grace,
let there be a perfect marriage between my two natures.
Let the two become one in You.

*TODAY, I AM GRATEFUL FOR:*_____
_____

GOD'S DAY 286 — *Seed of God*

Remember, _____,
(speak your name aloud)

—*you have sprung forth from the seed
of God deep in your soul, and your soul*

is flowering beautifully.

Make no judgment of yourself or your life based on outer struggles. Many flowers must push up and grow through stony soil and hard places.

Roses as well as nettles, orchids as well as skunk cabbages—are all beautiful in their own right, growing where they need to grow.

It is only your judgment of them that is wrong. Do not misjudge yourself or others, for you are each growing and flowering according to your individual expression.

Bloom where you are.

Water your soul with love and admiration and give it the sunshine of your faith in its divine origin and beauty.

*Today, I water my soul with love,
and give it the sunshine of my faith.*

TODAY, I AM GRATEFUL FOR: _____

_____

GOD'S DAY 287 — Prosperity

Remember, _____,
(speak your name aloud)

*—you can only receive to the limit of your mental container—
your consciousness.*

What size container are you taking to the well—a cup or a barrel?

The universe is capable of supplying in any amount, but if you only believe you are worthy of receiving a little amount, that is exactly what you will receive—

*—a little bit of wealth,
—a little bit of health,
—a little bit of love.*

If you are only willing to give and share a little amount that is all that can come back to you.

Are you saying "Thank you" in advance, knowing that your good comes in God's own timing, not yours.

Finally remember:

*"According to your faith
(and your giving and your gratitude)
shall it be done unto you."*

TODAY, I AM GRATEFUL FOR:_____

GOD'S DAY 288 — *Divine Mystery*

Remember, _____,
　　　　　(speak your name aloud)

You are part of the eternal mystery called God.

A mystery—invisible except as seen in the eyes of an infant looking at its mother, and in the eyes of the mother looking at her child.

Unknowable except in that instant flash of inner knowing.

Everywhere present as your spirit visits with a departed loved one in your dreams.

You are part of the divine mystery—present here and now, yet having always been so since the beginning of time.

There are powers, and heights and depths to your soul that you have yet to explore in this lifetime—and that you may never truly know because your soul is part of that greater unknowable Mystery.

You will never fully know how beautiful and powerful you truly are. You have no idea of how much love you are capable of expressing, because you have no idea of the inexhaustible Love that is God, at the heart of you. This is all part of the mystery that you are, and that God is. Rejoice today, and be humble in that mystery!

In your meditation contemplate this thought:

I am part of the beautiful, unfathomable Mystery that is God.

TODAY, I AM GRATEFUL FOR: _____

_____

GOD'S DAY 289 — *Returning*

Remember, _____,
            (speak your name aloud)

" *. . . in returning and rest shall you be saved;*
in quietness and confidence shall be your strength . . ."
Isaiah 30:15.

Return to your Source, to Spirit within.

Take time now to meditate and "rest in the Lord."

In that quietness you shall renew your strength.

Take these words with you as you enter the silence:

In quietness and confidence
I realize that Christ is ever in the midst of me.

In quietness and confidence
Christ is renewing and restoring me.

I am serenely confident and Christ-assured.

*TODAY, I AM GRATEFUL FOR:*_____

_____

GOD'S DAY 290 — *Designated Driver*

Remember, _____,
>   (speak your name aloud)

—to choose who will be your "designated driver" today.

Who will you put behind the wheel of your life today— your fear-based ego, or your love-based Higher Self?

Ask yourself today:

> *Who is in charge of my day?*
> *Who is driving my actions?*
> *Who is making the decisions about my day's activities—*
> *and what I will say on the phone calls I make,*
> *and at the meetings I will attend?*

You have the power to choose your "designated driver."

Will it be your Higher Self, or your fear-based ego? If you do not make a conscious choice, your ego will drive by default, taking you down roads you don't want to go.

Today, put your Higher Self in charge of your day!

Hold this thought during the day:

> *Lord, you are my designated driver today.*
> *Drive, act, speak and work through me.*

TODAY, I AM GRATEFUL FOR: _____

_____

GOD'S DAY 291 — God Is Spirit

Remember, _____,
               (speak your name aloud)

           —God is Spirit.

That Spirit lives in you as you, animates your body temple, and thinks its highest thoughts in your mind.

God is not a person, except as personalized and individualized in you as the Christ Presence.

In your quiet time now meditate on the ancient Gaelic prayer:

> *O Christ thou Son of God*
> *Live Thou thy life in me,*
> *Live Thou thy love in me,*
> *Be Thou made flesh in me,*
> *Do Thou thy will in me,*
> *I will have no will but thine,*
> *I will have no life but thee.*
> *O Christ, thou son of God, my own eternal self.*

*TODAY, I AM GRATEFUL FOR:*_____

_____

GOD'S DAY 292 — *Wait on the Lord*

Remember, _____,
(speak your name aloud)

"...they that wait upon the lord shall renew their strength;
they shall mount up with wings as eagles;
they shall run, and not be weary;
and they shall walk, and not faint."
Isaiah 40:31

"Wait on the Lord."

Say, *"Lord, I'll be your server today."*

Serve that Presence who continually serves you.

"Wait on the Lord."

Patiently wait and listen for his coming.

Put the porch light on in your heart.

"Wait on the Lord,"

—in meditation for the Lord's words.

Wait for the Lord's love and joy to fill your heart.

TODAY, I AM GRATEFUL FOR: _____
_____

GOD'S DAY 293 — *Stilling the Storm*

Remember, _____,
                    (speak your name aloud)

> *—when the storms of life threaten to overwhelm you,*
>   *hear the Christ within say, "Peace, be still."*

Just as Jesus spoke those words to still the storm on the Sea of Galilee, so you can speak them to quiet the fear in your heart.

Jesus and his disciples were out in a fishing boat during a storm and the waves were swamping the boat. Jesus was asleep in the stern. The disciples became panicky and cried out, "Master, do you not care if we perish?" Immediately Jesus awoke and stilled the storm. *"Peace, be still."*

Jesus represents your spiritual awareness of God's Power and Presence within you awaiting your call in times of trouble.

Ask yourself in meditation:

> *Is the Christ asleep in me?*
> *Why have I not called on Him sooner*
>   *to still the storms of my life?*
> *Is my own Indwelling Lord just a passenger in my ship of Life,*
>   *or do I call upon the Lord through daily prayer and*
>   *meditation?*

When you feel you are about to drown in the storm of life's problems, remember to call upon your inner Christ to take charge, and declare: *Peace Be Still!*

*TODAY, I AM GRATEFUL FOR:*_____

_____

GOD'S DAY 294 — All Related

Remember, _____,
                 (speak your name aloud)

           —you live in a hall of mirrors.

Everywhere you look—every person, every creature of creation—is reflecting back to you a part of yourself. It is showing you that you are part of the whole, part of the universal Allness.

You have a kinship with all life.

As the native American Lakota Indians say:

Mitakuye Oyasin—we are all related in the Great Spirit—all related at the planetary and spiritual level.

Our purpose in life is to attain a consciousness of that Oneness.

Love your neighbor, as well as your enemy, because he is you, and you are he, and you are one.

Hold this thought today:

    I am part of all there is, one with all life.

TODAY, I AM GRATEFUL FOR: _____

_____

GOD'S DAY 295 — *Spiritual Growth*

Remember, _____,
　　　　　　(speak your name aloud)

—you are enrolled in a Masters School,
and Life wonderfully presents you with whatever
is needed for your spiritual growth.

It is through the so-called problems you work through in life that you achieve self-mastery.

Every crisis overcome builds your faith muscles.

If you run from fear it will only meet you farther down the road in another form or face. Meet it with courage and ask for its message.

In your meditation dialogue with it.

Write the questions:

Fear, who are you, and where do you come from?
Who or what do you represent in me?
What message do you have for me?

Become quiet and receive intuitive answers. The fear will reveal its origin and identity to you so that you can then transform it with Christ Truth and Love.

As you meet fear with faith, you will have mastered one more course in the Masters School of life..

Today, dialogue with your fears.

*TODAY, I AM GRATEFUL FOR:*_____

GOD'S DAY 296 — *Home School*

Remember, _____,
(speak your name aloud)

—the personal ego is a con man.

Be careful of its smooth talk and its false confidence.

The ego promises you love, when in truth it doesn't know the meaning of the word, and has never experienced it.

It promises to lead you in the way of your good, when in truth it is lost in materiality and cannot find its way out of its hall of mirrors.

It is you that must rescue it. It is you that must take this little lost child by the hand and lead it home to God.

It is you that must take over its education and "home school" it until it learns the way of the Lord—the way of truth, of life, and of love.

Take yourself in hand now—your little lost personal self and lead it home to God in meditation.

Let your prayer be:

Take my hand, little lost self.
I will lead you back home to the Father's house
of safety, peace, and love.

TODAY, I AM GRATEFUL FOR: _____

_____

GOD'S DAY 297 — *Holy Moments*

Remember, _____,
　　　　　　(speak your name aloud)

—this very moment is a Holy Moment.
Breathe in the beauty of it and be grateful.

This very moment God's loving Presence is with you, in you, living as you.

Be awake and aware of who you really are—

—God's beloved

—God's instrument

—God's opportunity to love, create, and express on Earth.

This very moment open yourself for that Infinite Love to flow through you.

Hold this thought in meditation:

Lord, in this Holy Moment, awaken me to your Presence.
Awaken me to the opportunities You have for me today.
Help me to know that every moment is a Holy Moment.

TODAY, I AM GRATEFUL FOR: _____

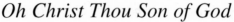

Oh Christ Thou Son of God

Oh Christ Thou Son of God,
heal the sick in me . . .

Cleanse the lepers in me—
—the unacceptable parts of my psyche . . .

Raise the dead hopes and dreams
and buried potentials.

As the Sun rises to light the Earth,
so let Thy Light rise in me
until there is no more darkness, anger or fear.

"Heal the sick, cleanse the lepers,
raise the dead, cast out devils;
freely ye have received, freely give."

Matthew 10: 8

GOD'S DAY 298 — Spiritual Internet

Remember, _____,
           (speak your name aloud)

    —to ask yourself:
"What are you posting on the cosmic 'Innernet'
    for all the world to see today?"

Just as there is a worldwide computer Internet linking vast bits of information, so there is a world-wide spiritual *"Innernet"*—an infinite network of spiritual, mental, and emotional intelligence and energy. As Jesus implied, we are all branches of the One Vine.

Research in prayer as well as mental telepathy shows how our thoughts and images are received by others on this spiritual *Innernet.*

Not a blessing or a curse goes forth from you that does not have its effect somewhere in the universe.

What are you sending forth today?

What are you posting on your cosmic website today for all the world to see?

*TODAY, I AM GRATEFUL FOR:*_____

GOD'S DAY 299 — *God is All There Is.*

Remember, _____,
                 (speak your name aloud)

   —you are part of all there is.

 —the wide-open spaces and the deep inner spaces.

 —the love in the eyes of your loved one,

 —and the anger in the heart of your enemy.

 You are part of all there is—and it is all yours to love, it is all yours to appreciate, and to transform with your Christ Light and Love.

 It is waiting for you to transform it.

 Remember, you are part of all there is, and all there is, is God.

 Meditate on this thought:

  I am part of all there is, and all there is, is God.

  Today, I know myself as part of God—
part of God's infinite Love, part of God's infinite Wisdom.

  From God I have all that I need
to live, work, and love today.
Thank You, God!

TODAY, I AM GRATEFUL FOR: _____

GOD'S DAY 300 — New Self Image

Remember, _____,
                    (speak your name aloud)

—you are who you believe yourself to be—
and unfortunately, that can be the cause of much
of your unhappiness.

You are made in the spiritual image of God (Good), but if you believe yourself to be something less than good, you are creating unhappiness for yourself.

Who do you believe yourself to be?

If you believe yourself to be a victim of long-ago abuses, then that image planted in the garden of the subconscious mind will continue to grow unhappy experiences for you—until you change that old image of yourself.

Realize, right now, that you are no longer that person. Create a new identity of yourself as a free, courageous, and victorious person.

Plant that new positive self-image in the garden of the subconscious, and it soon will be growing happy situations in your life that will confirm your new belief about yourself.

Right now, hold this thought:

No longer am I that victim.
I am a courageous and confident person
I am special and I am worth loving!

*TODAY, I AM GRATEFUL FOR:*_____

GOD'S DAY 301 — *Persistence*

Remember, _____,
             (speak your name aloud)

—to be persistent in prayer.

Have you ever seen a little dandelion plant pushing up through a crack in the concrete? What tremendous power in that tiny plant to break concrete!

Have you ever seen a tree growing up out of a rock that it has split over years of obeying its life's urge?

There is tremendous power in persistence—the tiny but continuous push toward expression.

That cherished desire you are working toward will yield to your persistent faith in its achievement.

Hold firm to seeing the accomplished desire in your mind's eye, and know in your heart that it is already so. That tiny seed of a desire will push up through the concrete of every obstacle.

*With God's help, I persist with faith
and push up through every obstacle.*

TODAY, I AM GRATEFUL FOR:_____
_____

GOD'S DAY 302 — *Expectations*

Remember, _____,
         (speak your name aloud)

—things and people are as they are,
and not as you want them to be.
Let go of expectations.

Too often we are like the monkey who sees a banana inside a jar. He reaches into the jar to grab the banana, only to find that he can't get his hand out.

Monkeys have been captured that way, for the monkeys tend to hang on to what they want.

Like the monkeys, we, too, hold on to expectations, people, possessions, and wrong beliefs that trap us.

Many parents see only what they want their children to be, they miss what their children really are, and are reluctant to accept that! Their hand is stuck in the banana jar of expectations.

The same is true for many husbands and wives—they don't really see and hear their spouse because of their expectations of how they think their spouse should be.

Today, let go of your preconceived expectations and beliefs. Experience the freedom of loving yourself and others just as they are—expressions of God.

Today, I let go of expectations of myself and others.
I accept the true and the beautiful hidden in everyone.

TODAY, I AM GRATEFUL FOR: _____

_____

GOD'S DAY 303 — *Healing*

Remember, _____,,
          (speak your name aloud)

      —to heal those old emotional wounds.

Wounds to the soul are as life threatening as severe wounds to the body. They bleed emotional energy.

Stop the bleeding from those emotional wounds by ceasing to dwell on them. Stop identifying with who and what you were at that time. You are not that person anymore.

Heal those old wounds now by bringing the antibiotic of Christ love and forgiveness to that old memory. Seal the wound so it bleeds no more by seeing yourself in a new way. Give yourself a new identity, a new description.

What new name will you give to yourself?

      Not (your old name)—the Victim,
      but (your new name)—the Victorious,
      the Beloved, the Confident!

Today, heal those old wounds and create a positive new you!

*TODAY, I AM GRATEFUL FOR:*_____

GOD'S DAY 304 — *First Things First*

Remember, _____,
       (speak your name aloud)

—*to ask your indwelling Lord:*

    "Why did I come into this lifetime, Lord?"

See what the response is.

Didn't you come to "sing your own song"?

Didn't you come in to do what you have been feeling deep down in your heart you always wanted to do and be—but never had the courage or opportunity to do? That is God's prompting. Have you been ignoring it?

Why is it that we put this most important thing last in our lives? Why do we let everything and everyone else take precedence—using up all our time and energy?

Get started today on whatever you came into this life to do!

Put it first in your life!

God is waiting for you to say Yes!

Today, I say Yes to_____.

Today, I say Yes to_____.

TODAY, I AM GRATEFUL FOR: _____

_____

GOD'S DAY 305 — *Free Yourself*

Remember, _____,
> (speak your name aloud)

> *—life is not meant to be lived in a box.*

If you feeling "boxed in" by the conditions of your life right now, break free with this meditation:

Imagine yourself sitting tightly cramped inside a box— knees against chest, head pressed down by the top of box. Feel your sense of desperation.

Ask yourself:

What conditions in my life are making me feel like this?

What or who has "boxed me in?"

Take a deep breath and say to yourself,

> *"I am more than these limitations.*
> *I am free by the power of my Indwelling Spirit."*

Now visualize yourself reaching up with your arms, pushing the lid off the box, and standing up. Break out the sides, and step free.

Declare*:*

> *I am free, praise God, I am free!*
> *No person, ideas, or conditions can bind me.*
> *I am free and ready for my good!*
> *Amen.*

You are free with the freedom of spirit!

*TODAY, I AM GRATEFUL FOR:*_____

_____

GOD'S DAY 306 — Divine Smile

Remember, _____,
 (speak your name aloud)

—the dark feelings you are feeling may not be yours.

You may be picking up on negativity emanating from those you are emotionally in tune with, or those in your soul group, or even from the collective unconscious of all humanity.

The dark feelings have come to you to be healed, because you have the spiritual understanding, the Love of God in your heart, and the divine Smile to transform them.

The Buddha is often portrayed as having a smile on his face. It is the divine Smile that dissolves all pain and suffering because he knows there is only God—perfect Love, Light and Peace—and all else is a lie and an illusion.

So remind yourself:

There is only God and all else is a lie.

As you close your eyes now, smile, and breathe the brilliant Light of God's Love into the dark feelings.

Do it several times, visualizing the darkness changing into light. Feel the darkness changing to peace.

Smile with the knowing that as you heal your own dark feelings, you are healing those of your soul group, and of all humanity.

TODAY, I AM GRATEFUL FOR: _____

_____

GOD'S DAY 307 — *Soul Lessons*

Remember, _____,
    (speak your name aloud)

—to treat every experience
as a soul learning experience—for it is.

When you are faced with a confusing and difficult situation, extract the good from it by asking:

What's the good in this for me?
What can I learn from this experience?
What good lesson can I learn here?
How can I use this to grow stronger in faith
and trust more strongly in God to bring good
from this situation?

As you truly seek and ask, you shall be shown the purpose of the challenge.

You will be given the deeper understanding to free you from the useless unnecessary suffering of the experience and enable you to extract the blessing from it.

Let your prayer be:

Lord, show me the soul lesson in this experience.

*TODAY, I AM GRATEFUL FOR:*_____

_____

GOD'S DAY 308 — *Centered and Poised*

Remember, _____,
           (speak your name aloud)

           —to center yourself in the peace of God.

Perhaps you have awakened very early today and felt the calm and peace of the morning hours. And then, as others began to rise and prepare for their day, you sensed the stress and tension as they hurried off to work.

As you begin to engage in your daily activities, take the following statement into your heart as you breathe deeply and slowly:

*I am centered and poised in the peace of God
and nothing can disturb the calm peace of my soul.*

Remember this prayer at work when the atmosphere around you is getting hyper and people around you are getting stressed. Take a deep breath and re-center yourself in the peace of God.

Centered in your own Indwelling Presence and Power, you will be unaffected by any negative vibrations around you. Instead, you will be a calming agent in the center of the storm.

*I am centered and poised in the peace of God
and nothing can disturb the calm peace of my soul.*

TODAY, I AM GRATEFUL FOR: _____

_____

GOD'S DAY 309 — *God is Greater*

Remember, _____,
(speak your name aloud)

—God is greater.

When you are confronted with a seemingly hopeless situation, know that *God is greater!*

Your own strength may be inadequate, but God can do what needs to be done.

Let go of the fear of what might be, and let God bring forth a miracle in you this day.

Remember, where you cannot, *God can!*

In your quiet time now, admit your own powerlessness, and surrender to the Power of God at work in and through you.

Let your prayer be:

Loving Power within me,
I admit my powerlessness in this situation.

I surrender myself and all my concerns to your Power
to bring about the best for my highest good.

I totally trust and rest in your care.
Your will be done.

*TODAY, I AM GRATEFUL FOR:*_____

_____

GOD'S DAY 310 — *Holy Vision*

Remember, _____,
          (speak your name aloud)

           —who you really are.

You have had tiny glimpses of yourself in times of great love, of prayer, and danger—times when your soul swelled to bursting with love and beauty. Times when you felt infinitely strong and unafraid.

The truth is that you are a spiritual being endowed with the power to bless, heal, and prosper.

You are a ray of the One Light, Love and Power.

You are an extension of the One into the world of form and manifestation.

You are all of these. Awaken out of your human sleep-walking state. Begin identifying with your true nature now, and rejoice.

You are that holy vision. See yourself that way now in a quiet moment of meditation.

Loving Lord help me to remember who I truly am—
a branch of the True Vine,
a child of the One Father,
with access to all that the Father has.

TODAY, I AM GRATEFUL FOR: _____

GOD'S DAY 311 — Perfect Peace

Remember, _____,
           (speak your name aloud)

> *"Thou wilt keep him in perfect peace,*
> *whose mind is stayed on thee:*
> *because he trusts in thee."*
> (Isaiah 26:3)

Let your mind be single-pointed, like a compass needle pointing north.

Personalize the above Bible verse as you let the compass needle of your mind swing to center on God. Take a deep, slow breath, and speak the following to yourself:

> *Thou wilt keep me in perfect peace,*
> *when my mind is stayed on You: because I trust in You.*

Let your mind return to its Source as you contemplate this next verse from Isaiah 30:15

> *In returning and rest shall ye be saved,*
> *in quietness and confidence shall be your strength.*

Again personalize the verse:

> *In returning and rest shall I be saved,*
> *in quietness and confidence shall be my strength.*

Draw in all scattered forces. Return to Center, to God, where there is quietness and confidence.

In a few moments you will find yourself calming down, your mind and heart in peace, as you trust in that abiding Presence.

TODAY, I AM GRATEFUL FOR: _____

_____

GOD'S DAY 312 — *Abundance*

Remember, _____,
(speak your name aloud)

—to make today "Abundance Day!"

Fill the coffers of your consciousness with divine ideas of God's infinite abundance.

Remind yourself that God is your instant, constant, and unfailing Supply on every level of living.

Spiritually, you are endowed with the divine DNA of God's nature—all that the Father has is yours to use and to share.

Mentally, you are supplied with divine ideas of creativity, beauty, and prosperity. Focus on these divine ideas and you will bring them into your life.

Emotionally, you are supported by God's unfailing Love that sustains you in every challenge and difficulty.

Physically, you are filled with God's radiant life, health, and energy.

Materially, you are richly and appropriately housed, clothed, transported, and supplied by the rich Substance of God.

Today, hold this thought:

Right now, this very moment, this very hour,
God is supplying my every need in the right way,
and I am grateful.

TODAY, I AM GRATEFUL FOR: _____

_____

GOD'S DAY 313 — God's Song

Remember, _____,
        (speak your name aloud)

—God wants to sing his song through you—
a song that is uniquely you.

The universe is music—every atom, every cell, every mineral, every plant is dancing to its own unique tune! And so are you!

Ancient legends say that God sang the world into creation, and that the seven days of creation were seven different marvelous songs. How beautiful! A musical note for each of the seven colors of the rainbow.

Listen and you will hear God's music all around you. In the wind chimes of the trees, in the song of the redbird, in the voice of your loved one speaking your name.

God wants to sing his song through you—a song that is uniquely you. Open your heart and let that song of life, love and joy, and creativity come forth!

Today, sing your song—the one God gave you to sing! Let your creativity play!

Let your prayer be:

Lord, sing Your Song through me today!

TODAY, I AM GRATEFUL FOR: _____

_____

GOD'S DAY 314 — *Seek, Obey, and Find*

Remember, _____,
> (speak your name aloud)

> *—stop seeking and you shall find.*

Have you been searching for something you mislaid in the house or at work? If so, you may have been looking everywhere but in the right place, and that right place is within yourself.

When Jesus said, "seek and you shall find…," There is a hidden word in there—"obey." Seek, and obey the promptings of the still small voice within you, and you shall find.

Stop seeking for a moment and become quiet. Stop the mind anxiously chattering advice about the next place to look, and simply ask:

> *Spirit, please tell me where it is.*
> *Show me where to find it.*

Let it be, and go do something else entirely unrelated. In a little while a quiet prompting will come to you. Obey it, and you shall find!

Seek, Obey, and Find!

TODAY, I AM GRATEFUL FOR: _____

_____

GOD'S DAY 315 — *Send Forth Your Thought*

Remember, _____,
            (speak your name aloud)

> *—your thoughts go before you like a messenger*
> *to announce your coming.*

Visualize the people you will be meeting today at work, your appointments, etc.

Send forth your thoughts and see yourself greeting them with goodwill and compassion, harmonizing every situation.

Set this as your spiritual intention and it shall be accomplished for you by the great Law of Cause and Effect—the Law of Karma.

Take a quiet moment now to hold this thought:

> *I send the spirit of goodwill and compassion*
> *before me on my path today.*

*TODAY, I AM GRATEFUL FOR:*_____

_____

GOD'S DAY 316 — *Moving Forward*

Remember, _____,
       (speak your name aloud)

   —*security is the ego's holy grail.*

   If you desire to move forward in life, you must dare to break out of your security shell and push the past behind you.

   Think of a baby turtle just breaking out of its shell.

   With its flippers it is doing the breaststroke, pushing its shell away behind it. It is sticking out its neck, and it is looking up with a quizzical smile on its face.

   Have the courage to stick your neck out, push the past behind you, and face the future with a smile!

   Break out of your shell and go for the Good that God has for you!

   Let your prayer be:

   *Lord, help me to break out of my ego shell of fear
       and self- limitations.*

   *Give me the courage to face the future with a smile
   and move forward to the new good you are preparing for me!*

TODAY, I AM GRATEFUL FOR: _____

_____

GOD'S DAY 317 — God is Your Parachute

Remember, _____,
  (speak your name aloud)

  —the words of an army paratrooper:

"you may believe that your parachute will open when you jump
out of the plane, but until you have faith and total trust, you
won't surrender yourself to the parachute and jump."

God is our parachute, and we have to reach the point of total trust.

Most of us operate on the belief level. We believe in God, but we don't actually totally trust God to provide for us until we have exhausted all other outside help.

As the expression goes, when all else fails, read the Instruction Book.

In the Book turn to the chapter on Psalms and read:

"Commit thy way unto the Lord; trust also in him;
and he shall bring it to pass."
  (Psalm 37:5)

Today, in your quiet time, commit your way unto the Lord.

*TODAY, I AM GRATEFUL FOR:*_____

GOD'S DAY 318 — *Slaying the Dragons*

Remember, _____,

      (speak your name aloud)

   —your problems are your fears reflected back to you.

Have you ever had a nightmare in which wild animals were threatening you?

They are a part of your psyche representing your fears and terrors.

When you are faced with those inner dragons that are so terrifying, know they are waiting to see how you will react to them. You actually are their master and they are really waiting for your love, your reassurance and comfort.

Close your eyes now in meditation. Call the most frightening fear or problem to mind now. Let it assume the character of an animal, if you choose.

Begin to soothe it as you would a frightened animal. Talk quietly to it, assuring and comforting it.

As it sees you calm down and lose your fear of it, so it will also calm down. Dialogue with it until you get its message.

Soon you will be at peace, and you will have healed yourself of that fear and solved the problem in your life that it represents.

Let your prayer be:

      Peace be still, there is nothing to fear,
          for God is here.

TODAY, I AM GRATEFUL FOR: _____

GOD'S DAY 319 — *Appreciation*

Remember, _____,
        (speak your name aloud)

—you will be happy, prosperous, and powerful
in proportion to your ability to appreciate
what is good in your life!

Sometimes you are so busy talking about what you don't have—about what's missing in your life—that you miss the good that is already here!

At the beginning of next month keep a 30 day *Blessing Calendar.* Use any calendar that has a space for writing.

Every night at the end of the day, enter the most significant blessing of the day—the one you are most grateful for that day.

This *Blessing Calendar* will keep you alert to the Good in your life. The blessings may seem insignificant to someone else, but the important thing is that you are building an attitude of gratitude that will act as a magnet to draw more good to you.

It will make you more alert to the blessings that God has for you that you might easily overlook.

Start your day with gratitude, and the rest of the day will take care of itself smoothly.

TODAY, I AM GRATEFUL FOR: _____

GOD'S DAY 320 — *Concerns*

Remember, _____,
>   (speak your name aloud)

>   *—tonight as you lay aside your clothes of the day,*
> *think also of laying aside the cares and concerns of the day.*

If you want to put on the same worry clothes again in the morning, that's your choice, but if you give them to God just before sleeping tonight, they will be gone by morning.

As you drop off to sleep, imagine handing a bundle of your concerns to your indwelling Christ to handle them for you.

Let your prayer be:

>   *Thank You, Lord,*
> *for taking care of these for me so I can sleep easily.*
> *I let go of them now and let you handle them for me.*

In the morning you will awaken refreshed and renewed!

TODAY, I AM GRATEFUL FOR: _____

_____

GOD'S DAY 321 — Rest

Remember, _____,
(speak your name aloud)

—as a wave sinks back to the ocean from which it arose,
so let your thoughts sink back to Source.

Let your wandering, troublesome thoughts sink back and rest in the peace of God within you.

To each thought that rises, simply ask:

Who is thinking these thoughts?

The answer will come: *"Me, I am."*

Ask: *Who am I?*

Again the answer *I AM* will spring into your mind.

Hold on to that *I AM*—the sacred Name of God within you—the Source of all peace and power—and meditate on it.

Breathe in slowly and deeply on "I."
Breathe out on "Am."
I . . . . . . AM
Rest in that I Am.
Rest in the silence.
Peace.

*TODAY, I AM GRATEFUL FOR:*_____

_____

GOD'S DAY 322 — Synchronicity

Remember, _____,

(speak your name aloud)

—to declare today to be a Divine Order Day!

Have you ever experienced one of those rare days when everything flowed in perfect order—

—when all the traffic lights were green, and the things you needed were right there when you needed them—

—and the people you needed to meet came into your life at exactly the right time?

That is a small sample of what happens when you get in tune with God's plan for your life.

To be in *Divine Order* is to be in synchronicity with the Higher Mind that knows what you have need of before you ask, and brings you into alignment with who and what you need for each day.

That is a *Divine Order* Day.

Today, get in the flow of that divine synchronicity by declaring *"Divine Order"* as you go about your day!

Let your thought be:

*Let Divine Order be established in all
my activities today.*

TODAY, I AM GRATEFUL FOR: _____

GOD'S DAY 323 — Watered-Down Faith

Remember, _____,

(speak your name aloud)

—to ask yourself:

Have I watered down my faith?

If you are experiencing turmoil and distress, it may be telling you that you have divided your faith between the problem and God.

You have watered down your faith.

Instead of seeing God as the Only Presence and Power, you are acknowledging another power—the power of the problem.

Take back the power you have given to the problem by believing in it, and place your full faith on God.

In your quiet time now, meditate on this truth:

There is only one Presence and one Power in the universe and in my life—God the Good!

Right now, this very minute this very hour God is taking charge and all is well.

*TODAY, I AM GRATEFUL FOR:*_____

_____

GOD'S DAY 324 — God's Hand

Remember, _____,,
        (speak your name aloud)

   —to take God's hand today.

God is always reaching out a hand to help you and guide you.

You can try to walk through the difficulties of the day by yourself if you choose, but that is the hard way— the way of the ego that always thinks it knows better.

Your pride and stubbornness can take you down a rough road.

Today, do things the easy way. Put your hand in God's hand and walk peacefully through your day.

In your meditation now place your hand in God's hand.

I place my hand in God's hand today.

TODAY, I AM GRATEFUL FOR: _____

_____

GOD'S DAY 325 — *Armor of Light*

Remember, _____,
(speak your name aloud)

—fear is contagious; you don't want to catch it.

Today, be aware of the negative vibes that may be coming your way from others, and choose not to take them on. Don't get caught up in their negativity.

Silently imagine putting on the armor of God's Light. From within that shield, silently whisper a simple "Bless you" under your breath to the people involved in that negativity.

Your actions will neutralize the atmosphere, and you will walk through the day impervious to any negativity around you.

Let your prayer be:

*I clothe myself safely around
with infinite Love and Wisdom.*

"Therefore take the whole armor of God . . . "
Ephesians 6: 13

*TODAY, I AM GRATEFUL FOR:*_____

GOD'S DAY 326 — *Acceptance*

Remember, _____,
          (speak your name aloud)

             —to love what is!

Learn to love what is. Love it just as it is.

Trying to change someone in your life to what you think they should be, won't work.

Holding back your acceptance or love only aggravates the situation. Instead, love and bless the holy Presence of God in them, beyond what you find hard to accept. That includes loving yourself just the way you are too!

Look with the eyes of God and see the perfection beyond the appearances.

Isn't that how you want others to look at you?

You want them to see through your outer faults and foibles to the beauty and goodness that lies latent in you—the Perfect Is-ness.

Today, remember to look past the outer
and love that Is-ness!

TODAY, I AM GRATEFUL FOR: _____

_____

GOD'S DAY 327 — Get in the Flow

Remember, _____,
  (speak your name aloud)
    —to get in the flow of God's Good.

Have you ever flown in an airliner over the desert, and seen a ribbon of green wandering through the barren land below?

It marks a river whose banks are lined with trees. Riverbanks are always green. They are nourished by the precious water they channel and pass along downstream. This is one of the secrets of having an abundant life.

The more you agree to be a channel for Spirit to flow through, the more your life become green and prosperous. The "green stuff" will flow!

Today, remember to open yourself to be a channel for God to bless the world through. With a thankful attitude find a way to pass along some of your good to others.

Let your prayer be:

Today, I get into the flow of God's Good!

*TODAY, I AM GRATEFUL FOR:*_____

GOD'S DAY 328 — *God is in Charge*

Remember, _____,

(speak your name aloud)

—God is in charge.

Which really means the Power of Ultimate Good is in charge.

Whenever you are beginning a new task, affirm, *"God is in charge."*

If you are anxious about meeting new people, silently state as you enter the room, *"God is in charge."*

No matter what challenge lies before you, remember to acknowledge the truth that *"God is in charge."*

Take a quiet moment now to close your eyes and move through the various areas of your life—family, career, health, finances, etc.—and in each one declare:

Right here, right now, God is in charge!
Only God's Good can come into my life!

TODAY, I AM GRATEFUL FOR: _____

_____

The Lord's Prayer of Divine Love

Our Father of Love,
which art in the heaven of Love,
Hallowed be thy Name of Love.

Thy Kingdom of Love come.
Thy Loving Will be done,
on Earth as it is in heaven.

Give us this day our daily bread of love
and forgive us our debts of love,
as we also have forgiven those whom
we feel owe us debts of love.

And leave us not in the temptation
of not loving others, as you have loved us,
but deliver us from the evils of conditional love.

For thine is the kingdom of love.
the power of love, and the glory of love forever.
Amen.

GOD'S DAY 329 — *Higher Frequency*

Remember, _____,
  (speak your name aloud)

—to ask yourself:

What am I listening to on my inner radio?

Close your eyes for a moment and tune in to the thoughts being broadcast in your mind. If you hear a lot of negative static, it's time to change the station.

Switch to a Higher Frequency.

From deep in your heart you can hear the whisper of the Higher Voice saying:

"Be strong and of good courage. I am with you.
I will guide your way. I will never leave you.
I am your shield and your strength.

Today, choose to listen to that Higher Voice.

Let it lead you and give you the strength you need for your day.

TODAY, I AM GRATEFUL FOR: _____

GOD'S DAY 330 — *Thanksgiving*

Remember, _____,

(speak your name

aloud)

On Thanksgiving, let your

prayer be:

Thank You, Father-Mother God, for Your Spirit in me.
No matter what is mine to meet in life,
I know I can be victorious,
for Your ever-present Spirit of Truth is guiding, strengthening,
and helping me.

I am never alone, for You are in me and with me,
and together we shall find a way through every challenge.

Your Spirit is my very life, and to the degree that I allow—
You live and express through me.

Help me, Spirit, to be a greater expression of Your life and
love, thereby bringing harmony and peace to my world.

May I always remember that You are the giver of every good
and perfect gift. . .and so I give thanks to You, Spirit,
on this day and every day.

Help me to remember to give thanks to other human beings,
for each one is an expression of Your life and love.

Thank You, Father-Mother God! Amen.

*TODAY, I AM GRATEFUL FOR:*_____

GOD'S DAY 331 — Boomerang

Remember, _____,
           (speak your name aloud)

     —*what goes around comes around.*

What are you sending out today?

What thoughts and intentions are you setting into motion on the great boomerang of life?

What old judgments and actions are coming back to meet you today? Will they be a blessing or a curse?

If they are unpleasant, meet them with love and forgiveness, as the loving father welcomed back his prodigal son.

Welcome back your prodigals—the consequences of your mis-sent thoughts and actions.

Ask forgiveness, then love them and release them.

What are you sending out today?

TODAY, I AM GRATEFUL FOR: _____

_____

GOD'S DAY 332 — Radiant Life

Remember, _____,
(speak your name aloud)

—to see yourself aglow with the radiant Life of God today.

In your meditation now behold that radiant life energizing, healing, and restoring you to perfect wholeness. See it glowing in every cell and organ of your body temple.

Know, in that inner place of knowing—the secret place of the Most High, that you are whole and strong!

Know that the perfect Christ pattern—the spiritual DNA of wholeness—is embedded in the every cell and atom of your body.

Your body temple is being recreated according to that pattern right now.

Today, hold this thought in perfect gratitude:

I am aglow with the radiant life of God,
and I am grateful!

TODAY, I AM GRATEFUL FOR:_____

_____

GOD'S DAY 333 — *Loving Presence*

Remember, _____,
           (speak your name aloud)

    —you live, move, and have your being in God,
      the Allness that surrounds and infills you.

Only in your mind can you feel separate from that All-pervading Goodness.

Only in your mind can you think of yourself as separate and alone. It is an delirium of the ego.

You are like the little child who is sick and delirious, calling for his mother, when all the time his mother is sitting by the bed holding his hand and whispering,

    "I'm here, I'm right here with you, my child."

God's loving Presence is always with you, night and day, whispering,

    "I'm here, I'm right here with you, my child."

Meditate on that loving Presence now, and know you are never alone.

TODAY, I AM GRATEFUL FOR: _____

_____

GOD'S DAY 334 — *Faith Muscles*

Remember, _____,
(speak your name aloud)

*—every challenge and difficulty is an opportunity
to build your faith muscles—*

—and to believe in that wiser, stronger Self which is waiting to be called into action and given charge.

In your quiet time now, let go of your little worry-prone self and invite your Higher Self to take charge!

Let your prayer be:

Lord, take charge of my day.

*See me safely though any challenges,
and make me mightier than circumstances.*

*Lift my spirit until I feel your joy,
your protection and your peace.*

*TODAY, I AM GRATEFUL FOR:*_____

_____

GOD'S DAY 335 — *Spiritual Amnesia*

Remember, _____,
   (speak your name aloud)

> *—you have already passed the final exam*
> *a thousand times before.*

Your soul already knows with All-Knowing Wisdom. Your soul already knows how to love with Unconditional Love.

You have already done all of that. You are a master of the universe, but you have forgotten.

You have forgotten that you have come here to play, to create, to express your divine talents, and to meet other masters.

But they too, have forgotten their mastery when they passed through the veil of forgetfulness into this Earth life. They too, have been hypnotized by the appearances of this space/time dimension.

So we have become each other's teachers—helping each other to re-learn the master lessons that we have forgotten, through the rough and tumble classroom of this Earth life.

It is time to remember and awaken from your spiritual amnesia and be the master that you are.

Today, hold the thought:

> *Today, I remember my true nature and I rejoice!*

TODAY, I AM GRATEFUL FOR: _____
_____

GOD'S DAY 336 — God's Will

Remember, _____,
(speak your name aloud)

—the four most important words of any prayer are:

"Thy will be done."

That is when we turn everything over to our Higher Power.

That is when we place ourselves and our desires and goals lovingly in the hands of the Father, knowing that it is the Father's good pleasure to give us the kingdom of all good.

Today, use *"Thy will be done"* as your mantra.

Repeat it throughout the day—making decisions, thinking about loved ones, driving, working, and in all your activities. You will be opening the way for God's good to come to you.

Today, I let the will of God work through me!

Today, I will to will the will of God!

Today I will to will the will of Good!

*TODAY, I AM GRATEFUL FOR:*_____

_____

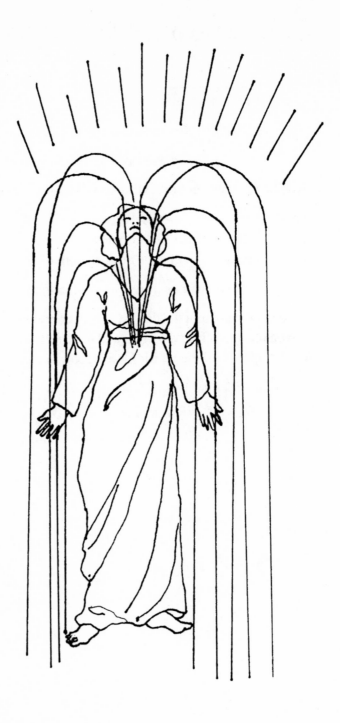

GOD'S DAY 337 — Fountain of Life

Remember, _____,
            (speak your name aloud)

   —God's Spirit is a fountain of life within you.

Close your eyes for a moment. Visualize a golden fountain of God's Life rising up from deep within you.

See it as a geyser of radiant light and health flooding up through the center of your body and spreading out to every part of your body as it rises.

Pull it upward as you inhale, and then exhaling, send its healing strength to every organ, muscle, and bone. Feel it rising up your spinal cord, healing your entire nervous system.

See it rising through the crown of your head and cascading down your body. Bathe in that golden fountain.

Repeat this seven times, visualizing it more vividly, and feeling it more strongly until you are completely filled with that golden light.

Hold to this prayer:

God's Spirit is a fountain of life within me.
I am renewed and restored in mind and body right now.
Praise God!

*TODAY, I AM GRATEFUL FOR:*_____

GOD'S DAY 338 — *Prayer for Children*

Remember, _____,
(speak your name aloud)

—to pray for the little children today.

Children are especially receptive to spiritual Truth being spoken to them.

Sit by their bed while they are sleeping, or if you are at a distance from them, then imagine yourself sitting by their beds.

Imagine surrounding them with a halo of God's Light as you speak softly to their souls:

I love you. You are God's beloved child.
You are now surrounded and protected
by a shield of God's Light.

No harm can come to you. You are safe in God's care.

God's Strength is strong within you.
You are strong in the Lord, and in the power of His might.

Mighty currents of God's healing love are flowing through you
now, healing and restoring you.

The Peace of God fills your heart and soul now.
You are at peace with yourself and all those around you.

You are God's beloved.

Rest in that Love and Peace now.

Leave them in God's care now.

TODAY, I AM GRATEFUL FOR: _____

_____

GOD'S DAY 339 — Self-Doubt

Remember, _____,
(speak your name aloud)

—to weed out self-doubt today!

Be done with it!

It eats away at your confidence, and undermines your progress. It blocks your vision of the true you—an unlimited expression of the Divine.

Be healed of your self-doubt now!

Be healed of your doubt that whispers 'you can't," when God shouts:

"Yes you can, because I can in you!

Let me do it through you!"

Be healed of your doubt about your eternal nature—about the infinitely powerful spirit of God that animates and empowers you.

In your meditation now, center on this truth:

I am healed of all doubt!
I can do all things through
the indomitable Spirit of God in me!
I can, because God in me can!

*TODAY, I AM GRATEFUL FOR:*_____

_____

GOD'S DAY 340 — *Divine Ideas*

Remember, _____,
                 (speak your name aloud)

—*the river of God runs by the door-*
        step of your mind,
waiting for you to put your canoe into
            the current.

Get into its flow. Divine ideas
sparkling like flying fishes are leaping to be caught as they
surface from the depths.

In the silence of meditation see that river of God flowing by.

Be still and catch those divine ideas flashing in the sun.

Be still now.
The Voice of Spirit is speaking.
Be still and listen.
Be still and know.

TODAY, I AM GRATEFUL FOR: _____

_____

GOD'S DAY 341 — *Dividing Your Power*

Remember, _____,
      (speak your name aloud)

   "A house divided against itself cannot stand."

   A mind with a problem is a mind divided.

   Half of its power is used to energize the problem, leaving only half for trusting in God as the solution.

   If you have a problem right now, cease wasting energy worrying about it. Put all your energy into knowing that with God all things are possible.

   Hold to the Truth that God is the Only Presence and Power—the only Reality in your life—and then do the work that is yours to do.

   In your meditation now, become still and affirm:

God is the one Presence and one Power at work in my life.

*The perfect solution is being worked out
on the deeper levels of my being.*

I relax, let go and let God take charge.

*TODAY, I AM GRATEFUL FOR:*_____
_____

GOD'S DAY 342 — *Lasting Value*

Remember, _____,
        (speak your name aloud)

    —to ask yourself:

What is really important today?

Not important in terms of work schedules, doctor appointments, or shopping errands, but what is really important in your life?

What is of lasting value?

What is important to your soul's growth and mastery?

What are you sharing of yourself today that will be a lasting legacy to those close to you?

Whatever these are, do them today.

Most important of all, share some love today—some act of friendship and compassion that will light the life of another.

TODAY, I AM GRATEFUL FOR: _____

GOD'S DAY 343 — *Abundance*

Remember, _____,
(speak your name aloud)

—your prosperity begins first in your mind, as does lack.

Jesus taught the great law of consciousness:

For to him who has more will be given,
and he will have abundance; but from him who has not,
even what he has will be taken away.
Matt. 13:12

To those that have a rich consciousness of God as Supply,
more will be given, but from those with a lack consciousness,
more will be taken away.

Clear your mind of thoughts of lack and replace them with
thoughts of God's abundance. Clear out resentment, jealousy
and self-condemnation that block the flow of God's abundance.

Open the flow today by asking God to help you forgive
yourself. Then forgive others that you feel have wronged you.
Finally, ask God to help you ask forgiveness of those whom you
feel you have wronged in some way.

When you have finished, write out the following statement
and place it on your mirror to look at every day.

Through daily forgiveness of myself and others,
I clear the channels of God's abundance.
New avenues of prosperity are opening to me now,
Thank You, God!

TODAY, I AM GRATEFUL FOR: _____

GOD'S DAY 344 — *Chosen One*

Remember, _____,
            (speak your name aloud)

—you are one of the chosen ones!

You did not come into this Earthly dimension by accident. You are here to be one of God's instruments to awaken humanity to its true nature.

You are here at this very time in history to take part in this great mission of moving humanity to its next level of spiritual development.

You are playing your part every time you express compassion to someone or some creature; every time you speak a word of encouragement to someone who is down, every time you are a peacemaker instead of a strife-maker— you are fulfilling your role in the uplifting of all humanity.

Do not underestimate yourself. Do not judge yourself by the appearances of your daily life. You are making a difference in the world!

Let your prayer be:

Lord, thank you for helping me
to make a difference today.

TODAY, I AM GRATEFUL FOR: _____

GOD'S DAY 345 — *Follow and Trust*

Remember, _____,
(speak your name aloud)

—Jesus' words,

"What is that to you, follow thou me."

Jesus advised his disciples to stop their worrying about the future, and simply follow him. Follow and trust.

Follow His way of knowing that with God all things work together for good. All is always as it should be.

Today, when you find yourself getting upset about some little annoyances, use that simple phrase:

"What is that to you?"

Is it really worth losing your peace about?

Will it really make any difference a hundred years from now? Let it go.

Think of how your Higher Self would view it, standing calm and unperturbed.

Hear that Master Self saying:

What is that to Me? It is nothing.
Follow Me in knowing that in the light of God's truth and love,
it is nothing.

Today, give those little ego annoyances to God. They are nothing.

*TODAY, I AM GRATEFUL FOR:*_____

_____

GOD'S DAY 346 — *Laughter*

Remember, _____,

(speak your name aloud)

—to laugh at yourself!

Can you see the divine comedy in your difficulties? The cosmic irony?

Send in the clowns!

Can you step outside yourself and with great humor see yourself—your foibles, and idiosyncrasies?

Can you see your eccentric traits and habits that would be so hilarious if a slapstick movie were made of you?

Right now, in the midst of this busy, hectic season, laugh at yourself!

Let that laughter drive away the blues and shift you into a higher perspective of yourself.

Spirit has a wonderful sense of humor!

Lighten up! All is as it should be!

TODAY, I AM GRATEFUL FOR: _____

_____

GOD'S DAY 347 — Be Patient

Remember, _____,
          (speak your name aloud)

> *—to practice patience today—*
> *patience with yourself,*
> *patience with others,*
> *patience in traffic,*
> *and at work.*

Behind every impatience is fear.

As small an impatience as being anxious that you might miss out on a parking space may cause you to get into a fender-bender.

Impatience in a healing crisis will erode your faith in God's power to heal.

The cure is to put God in charge of your day, from finding parking spaces, to the greater personal crises that you may be facing.

Whenever you are beginning to feel impatient, take a slow deep breath, and tell yourself,

> *Patience,_____(your name)*
> *God is in charge and all is well.*

*TODAY, I AM GRATEFUL FOR:*_____

GOD'S DAY 348 — *The Pulse of God*

Remember, _____,

       (speak your name aloud)

      —the very pulse of God is within you.

Sit quietly and put your finger on your pulse.

Feel that rhythm of life coursing through your veins. It is the very Life Pulse of God in you.

In your meditation now, silently chant *Praise God* to the rhythm of every beat;

      Praise...God, Praise...God, Praise...God.
      I praise the sacred life of God in myself.

Feel yourself taking an involuntary sigh as you relax into that sacred rhythm.

Know the life of God is strong within you.

Let your prayer be:

      The Life of God is strong within me.

TODAY, I AM GRATEFUL FOR: _____

GOD'S DAY 349 — *Let Your Old Self Die*

Remember, _____,
(speak your name aloud)

> —*to have a mock funeral service*
> *for your old self once a month.*

Let your old self die with a lily in your hands.

Let all your old fears, blames, guilts, and limiting beliefs die.

Lie there and say—

> " *Today, I let my old self die.. may it rest in peace.*"
> "*I let my old fearful self die so that the Christ can live in me.*"

Next, have a resurrection ceremony in which you proclaim—

> *Today this very moment*
> *I am born a new person in Christ . . . whole and free!*

In your meditation today have that mock funeral service and let your old self die.

Let the new you be resurrected.

During the month, whenever you find yourself worrying about something tell yourself—

> "*That died yesterday.*
> *Today is a brand new day with a brand new me!*"

*TODAY, I AM GRATEFUL FOR:*_____

GOD'S DAY 350 — *God's Rest Stop*

Remember, _____,
(speak your name aloud)

—to shift into 4-wheel drive when the going gets tough.

Do you remember driving through mountains and coming upon a scenic overlook where you pulled off and enjoyed the spectacular view? You could look back down the winding road that you just climbed.

In your meditation today, pull off the road and look back down the mountain of life that you have climbed. Gain perspective on your life and see that despite the detours, and the rough places, you have come a long way up.

Your life has a purpose and a beauty of its own that you couldn't see when you were rounding the blind hairpin turns, or in deep valleys of despair.

Rest in God's Rest Stop now. Take a deep breath and remind yourself that you are loved and you are safe, and God is guiding you on the long road ahead. Shift into spiritual 4-wheel drive and trust God with all four parts of your nature.

Trust spiritually by meditating on that loving Presence of God to see you safely through.

Trust mentally by keeping your thoughts on God for wisdom and guidance on your journey.

Trust emotionally by feeling God's Love filling your heart with courage.

Trust physically by acting in faith that God is your health and strength unfailing quick.

TODAY, I AM GRATEFUL FOR: _____

GOD'S DAY 351 — *Flip the Box*

Remember, _____,
                (speak your name aloud)

—life is not always as you see it to be.

The diagram is like a situation in life—it contains both the problem and the solution within it.

Life will always deliver to you according to your attitudes and how you view it.

There are two or three possible illusions in the drawing. You may see the box "open" at the top, or perhaps at the side.

Blink your eyes, and shift your gaze back and forth until your perspective suddenly shifts and you can see the box open in a new way. You have "flipped the box."

Are you letting your negative attitudes "box" you into seeing only one view of troublesome situation?

Ask,

> *"How would my fearless Higher Self see this situation? What is the good hidden here?"*

As you ask this, your perception shifts from the problem to the higher perspective. You see the situation or the person in a new way. You will have "flipped the box."

TODAY, I AM GRATEFUL FOR: _____

_____

GOD'S DAY 352 — *Shadow Self*

Remember, _____,
　　　　(speak your name aloud)

　—your shadow self holds a golden treasure for you.
　Dive into its dark depths and retrieve it.

Every quality that you deny or dislike about yourself is the shadow side of a beautiful and desirable quality that you are endowed with by your Creator. It is the rough exterior ore that hides within it the gold of your character.

In order to refine the gold hidden in your undesirable qualities, you must first acknowledge that you have them. Bring them up from the dark cellar where they are hidden and offer them to the fire of God's love to be refined.

　Lord, here is my mind—refine it of its fears,
　　　　its foolishness and ignorance.
Bring forth the pure gold of faith, wisdom, and understanding.

　Lord, here is my will—refine it of its stubbornness
　　　　and contrariness.
　Bring forth the pure gold of cheerful willingness
　　　　and obedience to Your will.

　Lord, here is my heart—refine it of its base passions,
　　　　resentments, and dissatisfactions.

　Refine it of its discouragements, and pride.
Bring forth the pure gold of pure love, forgiveness, patience,
　　　　humility and quiet joy.

TODAY, I AM GRATEFUL FOR: _____

_____

GOD'S DAY 353 — Gratitude

Remember, _____,
     (speak your name aloud)

   —never underestimate the power of a single glance,
       or an encouraging smile.

Ask yourself:

Who are the people who inspired me, who gave me a "leg-up" when I needed it?

Who encouraged me and believed in me?

Who were the persons with whom I really didn't get along—who were really quite a trial to me but caused me to grow, although unwilling at the time?

Run the movie of your life backwards to your childhood and search there. Search the scenes from home, school, and neighborhood. Search your teenage years, your work years.

The obvious benefactors stand out, but look for the lesser known, the strangers who touched your life but once and made a difference. All of these deserve your blessings and thanks.

In your meditation now, bring all of these into the spotlight of God's Love and express your gratitude.

TODAY, I AM GRATEFUL FOR: _____

_____

GOD'S DAY 354 — All The Time You Need

Remember, _____,
          (speak your name aloud)

   *—Christmas can be for you whatever you name it to be,
   hectic and materialistic, or peace-filled and joyous.*

If the pressures of shopping and preparing for the Christmas season is squeezing the joy out of Christmas, pause in the midst of the rush and remind yourself:

*I have all the time I need to do what needs to be done by me.
I work efficiently and joyously, as I draw on
God's strength and patience to sustain me.*

Take a deep breath and let that strength seep into your soul.

Let your holidays truly be holy days—filled with God's Peace and Light. It's up to you!

God is blessing you right now with peace!

TODAY, I AM GRATEFUL FOR: _____

_____

GOD'S DAY 355 — Giving

Remember, _____,
          (speak your name aloud)

    *—to practice patience with yourself and everyone else
    caught in the exhausting rush of gift shopping.*

In the midst of your thinking of those that you are going to give to this Christmas, think especially of giving a blessing to those tired clerks who serve you in the Christmas shopping rush.

When you are shopping, remember to give a warm smile or kindly word to the salespersons.

Bless them silently as they work to handle the long lines of customers.

Your smile and kindness may be just the gift they need to carry them happily through their day.

    Today be God's blessing agent!

TODAY, I AM GRATEFUL FOR:_____

GOD'S DAY 356 — *Help at Hand*

Remember, _____,
　　　　　(speak your name aloud)

　　　　　　—you do not walk alone.

In the anxiety of trying to find your way to your flight in the confusion of a crowded airline terminal, remember there is a loving Presence walking beside you.

Remember to say to that Presence:

"I could use a little help here, please."

Suddenly you will see the right way to go. Suddenly you will be guided through the corridors, through security, and know that you are safe and in charge. Yet not you, but the Presence walking beside you is in charge, and all is well.

Thank You, Spirit, for walking beside me
and guiding my way today.

TODAY, I AM GRATEFUL FOR: _____

_____

GOD'S DAY 357 — Discouragement

Remember, _____,
        (speak your name aloud)

"The people that walked in darkness have seen a great light;
they that dwell in the land of the shadow of death,
upon them has the light shined."
Isaiah 9:2

If your heart is dark at this time; if Christmas holds no promise of joy for you, take a moment to sit quietly in your darkness.

Close your eyes and let yourself feel those dark feelings. Perhaps the discouragement you feel is yours, but it may be you are picking up that of a family member or a close friend, or perhaps it the sadness of the Earth before the return of the Light.

Wait peacefully and in a little while you will be aware of a loving Presence sitting with you in the darkness of your despair. It is the Presence of the Holy One waiting to be born in you—the Holy One waiting for the first gleam of the Christ Star to appear in the heavens.

Watch and wait. A small light appears and grows stronger and brighter. Let it grow and fill your heart. Let it grow until it surrounds you and dispels the darkness.

Breathe in that Holy Light. Breathe in that Love. Breathe in that Joy. Rejoice that the Light of the World has come to lift you out of your darkness.

Take your Light now and light the lives of those still in the darkness—light their lives with your love, your concern, your gift. Let your Christ Light shine.

*TODAY, I AM GRATEFUL FOR:*_____

GOD'S DAY 358 — *Christ Star*

Remember, _____,

(speak your name aloud)

—the Star of Bethlehem,
the Star of Christ Light and Love.

Today, use the Star's love and power
to bless and heal yourself or a loved one.

Sit quietly and imagine the Star
above your head shining down upon you
and enveloping you with its Light.

Breathe its healing Light and Love into your heart and let
it radiate to every part of your body temple.

Let it shine on any particular part of your body needing
healing—penetrating into every atom and cell. See that area
glowing with the radiant Life of God—whole and perfect.

For a loved one, see them in the center of the Star—
surrounded and infused with that perfect Light and Love.

For yourself know that:

The Peace, Light, and Love of the Christ Star
is shining in my heart now.

TODAY, I AM GRATEFUL FOR: _____

_____

GOD'S DAY 359 — *Holy Night*

Remember, _____,
(speak your name aloud)

—your heart is the manger of the Christ child.

O Christ
of the manger,
You came as a helpless Babe!
All-Power of the Universe—
lying there in human form!
In me, too, is this divine Power—
locked in a garment of flesh.
Show me, O precious Babe,
How to release my imprisoned splendor, as You did!
All eyes are on You, O Christ!
And so must it be for us!

For You represent our indwelling Christ—gentle, lowly—
seemingly helpless as a baby, yet All-Power in potential!
And so as I focus on You, Your presence within me,
As I nurture Your spirit inside me,
You will grow "in wisdom and stature" in my being;

But, in Truth,
it will be my awareness of Your presence that will grow.
For You are the eternal Christ!
You change not!
You simply change the lives of those who acknowledge
and welcome You. And they (and I!) are transformed!
We become Christed beings!
So let it be with me, Lord—in me, Lord!
It is never too late to begin!
It is always the right time to be born!
So be born in me this very day,
O Christ—
my Christ—
this Christmas Eve.

GOD'S DAY 360 — *Wonderful Counselor*

Remember, _____,
          (speak your name aloud)

"for unto us a child is born,
unto us a son is given: and the government shall be on his
shoulder; and his name shall be called Wonderful Counselor,
the everlasting Father,
the Prince of Peace."
Isaiah 9:6

You have received the greatest gift that God has to give—
the Christ Child in the manger of your heart.

Now the greatest gift you can give God in return is the
life-long commitment to love that Child and raise and nurture
that Child until He grows strong within you.

Then let the government of your life be upon His shoulder.

He is the Wonderful Counselor—God's precious gift to
you.

Be eternally grateful and rejoice!

TODAY, I AM GRATEFUL FOR: _____

_____

GOD'S DAY 361 — *After-Glow*

Remember, _____,
 (speak your name aloud)

> *—after the Light has come,*
> *after the joy of Christmas subsides—*
> *rest in its afterglow.*

Let that glow stay with you as you resume your routine living—let it lighten your daily tasks.

That Christmas love has changed you and you are not quite the same person you were before Christmas.

Your heart has opened under the warmth of the gifts of love that were expressed to you.

The unexpected Christmas card, the surprise gift, the phone call from someone that you have been estranged from—all have touched you at soul depth.

The Star has left its Light in you.

Let it shine in you the rest of the year and beyond.

The Christ Child is beginning to stir and awaken in your heart. You have looked into His eyes and you will never be the same again.

TODAY, I AM GRATEFUL FOR: _____

_____

GOD'S DAY 362 — Be Grateful

Remember, _____,
>   (speak your name aloud)

There are those who love you. Be grateful.

There are those who seem to be your enemies, but are actually your teachers.

Be grateful.

There are those who would put you down and seem to be obstacles in your path, but they only serve to strengthen and build your faith muscles.

Be grateful.

They are all waiting to meet you on your pathway today— enemies and angels alike.

Be grateful.

How will you meet those on your path today?

Your attitude will empower you or betray you.

Let your prayer be:

> *I am so grateful!*

*TODAY, I AM GRATEFUL FOR:*_____

_____

GOD'S DAY 363 — *The Father Within*

Remember, _____,
             (speak your name aloud)

*—to get your little self out of the way today
                so Spirit can express.*

Step aside and remind yourself of the words of Jesus:

*"Of myself I can do nothing...
it is the Father within me that does the work."*

Let go of fearing that the task you are facing today has to be done by you alone—with your own limited skills and strength.

Where you can't, God can.

Let your prayer be:

*Lord, speak through me today, work through me,
love through me, heal through me.*

TODAY, I AM GRATEFUL FOR: _____

_____

GOD'S DAY 364 — *Growth*

Remember, _____,
        (speak your name aloud)

  —you are not the same person you were a year ago, or six months ago, for you have expanded your insight and awareness!

Just as trees in the springtime bring forth new buds that unfold and blossom beautifully, so your soul is blossoming beautifully too.

You are an ever-renewing, ever-unfolding expression of infinite life! Give thanks for your unfoldment!

If people from your past try to hold you to what you *were,* give thanks for the truth of that statement, because you *were* that person, but you are not that person anymore. You have grown greatly since then! You are a new person with infinite possibilities!

Dare to be that new person today!

In your quiet time now, visualize yourself being that new person.

Feel what it feels like. Feel the freedom of being that new person, grounded in Christ confidence, strong and capable, loving and wise.

Hold the thought:

> *Today, I leave the old self behind.*
> *I am a new person in Christ.*

TODAY, I AM GRATEFUL FOR: _____

GOD'S DAY 365 — *Burning Bowl*

Remember, _____,
         (speak your name aloud)

    —to travel light into the new year.

Today, get rid of the baggage of mind and heart accumulated in the closets of your soul over the past year.

Travel light *mentally* into the new year by clearing out the inner trash of old worries, and self-doubts.

Travel light *emotionally* by getting rid of the heavy baggage of grief, fear, and resentments.

Travel light *physically* by detoxifying your system. Travel light *materially* by releasing burdensome things.

In your meditation now, prepare for the new year by participating in a burning bowl experience. Mentally scroll back through the past year.

Ask yourself: *What burdens am I carrying in my heart that I want to be free of? What regrets of the past? What fears of the future? What old wounds and unforgiveness am I carrying? Who do I need to forgive or ask forgiveness of?*

Write them down. Then write this statement:

*I now surrender these to the refiner's fire of Christ Love
and forgiveness. I now let go and fully forgive.
I now let go and fully release.
Through the fire of Christ Love I now am free and fully forgiven. Praise God!*

Burn your notes now in a burning bowl and release them to God.

TODAY, I AM GRATEFUL FOR: _____

_____

I SURRENDER

Oh, Love
that would not let me go,
down through the ages,
I surrender.

Oh, Light that would not leave me in the dark,
down through the ages, I surrender.

Oh, Angel that followed me down through the ages,
not out of duty or assignment,
but out of the joy of seeing me unfold . . .

Oh, Thou who knew my destiny.
Oh. Voice who called to me though I would not listen,
down through the ages . . .

Oh, Thou Divine Mother who gave birth to my soul,
Who believed in me when I did not,
when I hesitated and said: "What have I to do with You, my
hour is not yet?"
who commanded the servants saying
"whatever he saith to you, that do."

Oh, Lord Jesus, Wayshower and Elder Brother,
the eldest of our family, who came back down the mountain
trail of eternity to lift me up where I had fallen,

—who showed me where to place my steps,
who counseled me and encouraged me—
who would not forsake me,
who said, "Step here and step there,"
and showed me the steps that You had cut in the mountain
for me to climb in . . .

Thank You for teaching me so that
I too can go back down the trail
to help others.
Amen.

End Notes

1. GOD'S DAY 3, Emma Curtis Hopkins, *Bible Interpretations, Second Series.* School of Christ Teaching, Alhambra, California, 1975, pp. 65-66, 71

2. GOD'S DAY 26, Transcendent *Treatment*, by H. B. Jeffery Unity School of Christianity, Unity Village, Missouri

3. GOD'S DAY 61, Angela Morgan, "Know Thyself" in Joseph Morris and St. Clair Adams (collectors)
It Can Be Done, George Sully & Co., New York, 1921, pp. 36-37

4. GOD'S DAY 94, *Invocation*, Charles Fillmore, Unity School of Christianity, Unity Village, Missouri

Prayer Index

Subject Index

(Subjects are referenced by God's Day number)

About the author

G. Richard Rieger is a metaphysical teacher, Unity minister, career and life coach.

He is the author of a popular career counseling book, *Inside Job, A Spiritual Approach to finding Your Right Work,* available through Amazon.com, Unity Online books, and book stores.

In *Remembering Who You Truly Are* he shares his twenty-five years of spiritual counseling wisdom for life's challenges.

Rieger has presented workshops on spiritual growth, self-esteem, and career counseling. For nine years he was program director at summer Unity spiritual retreats in Colorado.

Before entering the Unity ministry, Rieger was a business executive for fifteen years. He was ordained a Unity minister in 1974. His wife, Marilyn was ordained in 1975. Together they served as co-ministers at Unity churches in Independence, Missouri, and Vero Beach, Florida.

He has been a frequent contributor to Unity Magazine since 1979. Excerpts from one of his articles appear in the book *Riches for the Mind and Spirit* by Sir John Marks Templeton.

His website, spiritlifting.com lists his books, and audio recordings. He is available for online counseling and career coaching through his website.

Printed in the United States
41710LVS00010BB/23